According to the Greek philosopher Socrates, we only learn those things that we have forgotten. If we follow his thinking, we must conclude that the discoveries which will change our lives for the better are hidden in our past.

Crystals are known for keeping records. Their basic substance forms the basis for computer memory chips. The most amazing piece of crystal in existence is the Mitchell-Hedges Crystal Skull. This artifact from an ancient civilization causes changes in all who come near it. People who have looked at pictures of this treasure have reported astounding experiences.

Discover now the awe and mystery that is the Crystal Skull. You will learn all the known facts on this piece of sculpture, so finely made that it cannot be reproduced with all of the technology available to the modern crystallographer. You will learn about its amazing powers, which have changed the lives of those who have examined it.

The most important thing about this Crystal Skull is that it has something to say to you! Speaking from tens of thousands of years ago, it has a personal message for you that is important to your survival, and the survival of the world in this New Age. We are on the brink of a major change in our existence. Will you survive these changes? You can take the advice of Socrates and discover the methods and techniques you'll need for the future from your past—by way of the Crystal Skull. When you learn and follow the message of the Crystal Skull, you will be able to survive, becoming the spiritually evolved person you were meant to be.

About the Authors

Alice Bryant began her interest in occult/esoteric fields when quite young. She developed a fascination for the Crystal Skull, and her years of study led her to Mexico and the Yucatan. She has lectured on the Crystal Skull throughout the country. She is a Science of Mind practitioner.

Phyllis Galde has been a student of metaphysics all her life, and is currently a personal magical student of Denning & Phillips. A schoolteacher for 16 years, she has worked with many New Age organizations including the Edgar Cayce A.R.E., Theosophy, and is a MariEl healer. She is currently senior editor at Llewellyn Publications.

To Write to the Authors

We cannot guarantee that every letter written to the authors can be answered, but all will be forwarded. Both the authors and the publisher appreciate hearing from readers, learning of your enjoyment and benefit from this book. Llewellyn also publishes a bimonthly news magazine with news and reviews of practical esoteric studies and articles helpful to the student, and some readers' questions and comments to the author may be answered through this magazine's columns if permission to do so is included in the original letter. The authors sometimes participate in seminars and workshops, and dates and places are announced in The Llewellyn New Times. To write to the authors, or to ask a question, write to:

Alice Bryant or Phyllis Galde
c/o THE LLEWELLYN NEW TIMES
P.O. Box 64383-092, St. Paul, MN 55164-0383,
U.S.A.

Please enclose a self-addressed, stamped envelope for reply, or $1.00 to cover costs.

ABOUT LLEWELLYN'S NEW AGE SERIES

The "New Age"—it's a phrase we use, but what does it mean? Does it mean that we are entering the Aquarian Age? Does it mean that a new Messiah is going to correct all that is wrong and make the Earth into a Garden? Probably not—but the idea of a *major change* is there, combined with awareness that the Earth *can* be a Garden; that war, crime, poverty, disease, etc., are not necessary "evils."

Optimists, dreamers, scientists . . . nearly all of us believe in a "better tomorrow," and that somehow we can do things now that will make for a better future life for ourselves and for coming generations.

In one sense, we all know there's nothing new under the Heavens, and in another sense that every day makes a new world. The difference is in our consciousness. And this is what the New Age is all about: it's a major change in consciousness found within each of us as we learn to bring forth and manifest powers that Humanity has always potentially had.

Evolution moves in "leaps." Individuals struggle to develop talents and powers, and their efforts build a "power bank" in the Collective Unconscious, the "soul" of Humanity that suddenly makes these same talents and powers easier to access for the majority.

You still have to learn the "rules" for developing and applying these powers, but it is more like a "relearning" than a *new* learning, because with the New Age it is as if the basis for these had become genetic.

Other Books by Phyllis Galde

Crystal Healing: The Next Step

Forthcoming Books

Skull Magic

Crystal Balls: Ancient and Modern

The Dream Crystal Divination Kit (*with Frank Dorland*)

Llewellyn's New Age Series

THE MESSAGE OF THE CRYSTAL SKULL

From Atlantis to the New Age

Alice Bryant & Phyllis Galde

1989
Llewellyn Publications
St. Paul, Minnesota, 55164-0383. U.S.A.

International Standard Book Number: 0-87542-092-3
Library of Congress Catalog Number: 88-45193

First Edition, 1989
First Printing, 1989

Library of Congress Cataloging in Publication Data

Bryant, Alice, 1924-
  The message of the crystal skull.

  (Llewellyn's new age series)
  Bibliography: p.
  1. Mitchell-Hedges skull. 2. Quartz
crystals-Miscellanea. 3. Psychical
research. 4. Occultism. I. Galde, Phyllis,
1946-. II. Title. III. Series.
BF1030.M57B78 1988   133.3'22   88-45193
ISBN: 0-87542-092-3

Cover Photo: Frank Dorland
Cover Design: Brooke Luteyn
Photos: Frank Dorland
Technical Consultant: Frank Dorland

Produced by Llewellyn Publications
Typography and Art property of Chester-Kent, Inc.

Published by
LLEWELLYN PUBLICATIONS
A Division of Chester-Kent, Inc.
P.O. Box 64383
St. Paul, MN 55164-0383, U.S.A.

Printed in the United States of America

Permissions

Joseph Arguelles, *Mayan Factor*

Francis Joseph, "The Face of the Crystal Skull"

Otto Muck, *The Secret of Atlantis*

Francis Joseph, "The Crystals of Atlantis"

Miguel Leon-Portilla, *Aztec Thought and Culture*

Frank Waters, *Mexico Mystique*

Laurette Sejourné, *Burning Water*

Acknowledgements

I wish to especially thank Frank Dorland for his unfailing moral support and enthusiasm without which this book would never have been wirtten. I am grateful to all my friends in the field of metaphysics for their appreciaton of the wonder of the Crystal Skull and their understanding of my fascination with it and to the many great researches of pre-Columbian Mesoamerican thought and culture on whose work I leaned so heavily. I especially appreciate the cooperation of Francis Joseph for his futher work with the Crystal Skull. Most of all, my appreciaton and gratitude goes to my family. Their loyal support and encouragement truly made this book possible.

—Alice Bryant

Dedicated To
My Kids:
Harold A, Linda, Becky, and Kelley

—Alice Bryant

Contents

Part One:

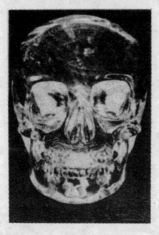

The Known Facts

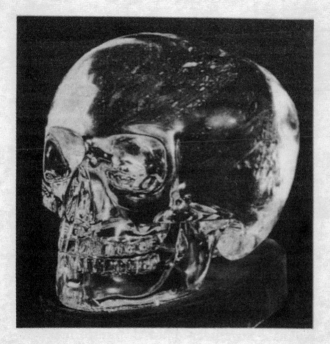

Mitchell-Hedges Crystal Skull

Chapter One

ORIGINS AND PREMISES

What exactly *is* the Crystal Skull?

It has been called the world's most mysterious artifact: a priceless, life-sized quartz crystal human skull, carved into a perfect likeness of a human head. Coming to us from uncharted ancient times, it cannot be duplicated even by today's advanced technology

Who made this amazing Skull, and for what reason was it made?

It is reputed to have unusual powers, and all who see or touch this Crystal Skull report unusual changes within themselves. Does the Skull have the power to heal or transform?

The Crystal Skull described in this book is commonly known as the Mitchell-Hedges Skull, because it was found by F.A. Mitchell Hedges' adopted daughter, Anna, while on an archaeological dig in British Honduras in the 1920s. Mystery and intrigue even surround the event of its discovery.

Not only is this Crystal Skull anatomically accurate, coming from an ancient time when such technical knowledge was supposedly unknown, but it would have been impossible to fashion it with the primitive tools early people had at their disposal.

There are two other *authenticated* ancient human-like quartz crystal skulls in museums. One, which is also life-sized, is in the British Museum of Man, and the other, smaller skull is in the Musee de L'Homme in Paris. These two skulls will be compared to the more finely crafted Mitchell-Hedges Skull.

Because quartz crystal cannot be carbon dated, there is no way of knowing how ancient this Crystal Skull might be. It is thought to be at *least* 12,000 years old, and some theories place its age in millions of years. The only sure way to determine its age would be to smash the Skull apart (destroying an exquisite artifact) in order to ascertain the age of the water inclusions trapped inside it. This, however, would only tell us the age of the crystal from which it was formed, not when the Skull itself was fashioned.

This amazing Crystal Skull is reputed to have miraculous healing properties and tele-pathic information concerning the origins of mankind. Many theorists feel it was either made or used in ancient Atlantis.

Why was a skull carved out of rock crystal anyway? Quartz crystal is an extremely hard substance (7 on the Moh scale), only slightly softer than diamond, and it is a very difficult medium to use in carving. One theory has it that the Skull was fashioned only after 300 years of patient craftsmanship in which sand and water were used to first smooth down the single piece of rock, and then the intricate details were carved into its surface.

Pioneer biocrystallographer Frank Dorland and his wife and associate, Mabel, carefully studied the Crystal Skull for six years. As art conservators, their first task was to authenticate the Skull and determine if it was a valid archaeological *objet d'art* and not a hoax. Their lengthy research yielded some fascinating results which you will read about here. The Crystal Skull literally taught them about the nature of crystal. They share their information for your enjoyment and learning.

You will learn the importance of quartz crystal, its ancient history, and its use in seeking spiritual awareness, health, happiness, and success. Beginning with the most famous piece of crystal in the world today, the Mitchell-Hedges Crystal Skull, you will meet the people most intimately involved with the Skull. You will be shown how the ancients used quartz crystal, and how these methods have evolved into modern techniques.

A scientific forensic restoration by modern experts shows how the living model may have looked. Here you will see that sometimes the truth is even stranger and more captivating than fiction.

An esoteric history of crystal use from the time of Atlantis to the present is traced. Because all of the crystal skulls described in this book were found in Meso-America, and because the skull motif was so prominent among the Mayan and Aztec worship, it is felt that this Crystal Skull was used extensively in rituals and worship among these cultures.

The myth of Quetzalcoatl (pronounced Ketzal-kwatl), the Mexican deity, is presented, plus the Skull's possible connection with Xolotl (pronounced Show-latl), the Dark Twin of Quetzalcoatl. Were the Toltecs (possibly the greatest artisans the known world has ever seen) capable of making the finely crafted Crystal Skull which was found by Mitchell-Hedges?

At one time it was thought to have been a "Skull of Doom," and anyone who looked at it would have bad luck or meet with an untimely death. It is hoped that this myth will be laid to rest in the spellbinding account you are about to read, and that you will understand the *real* purpose of the Skull, and not see it as it has sometimes been portrayed—a morbid curiosity.

By reading this book you will learn the value the Skull has for each and every one of us. It is hoped that you will come to see the Skull as an object of beauty, representing wisdom and the endless cycle of birth, death, and everlasting life.

The information you are about to read here

plus the captivating photos which are included in *The Message of the Crystal Skull* will show *you* how to obtain wisdom and knowledge directly from the Skull itself.

It is not necessary to be in the presence of the Crystal Skull to learn from it. By meditating on a picture of the Skull or imaging it in your mind, you can bring about some startling revelations in your consciousness—*if* you allow it. Information stored in this "crystal computer" can be accessed by your subconscious. It is waiting there, ready to be tapped by the storehouse of wisdom you have accumulated from the collective unconsciousness in its countless centuries of recording experiences on this planet.

F.A. Mitchell-Hedges on grounds at his home at Farley Castle near Reading, England.

Chapter Two

DISCOVERY AT LUBAANTUN

As a young boy in London, "Mike" Hedges only wanted to explore. He disliked school. He was happy only when he was reading adventure stories about faraway places. He was especially fascinated with tales of the ancient civilizations of Central America—the Mayans, Aztecs and Toltecs.

Not until he later realized his dreams to be an explorer and archaeologist would he be happy. Amassing a fortune and then losing it didn't even give him much satisfaction.

He had a belief in the legendary civilization of Atlantis, and he thought he could find remnants of it in British Honduras. An uncanny sixth sense was responsible for most of Mitchell-Hedges' archaeological finds. In British Honduras, the discovery of a rock carved with Mayan symbols urged him on to find the city he intuitively felt was there.

As a grown man he finally found himself in British Honduras. Would this be the realization of his dream of finding a lost civilization?

The jungle was incredibly hot and humid. In the seemingly endless struggle, he and his party had put up with bad food and worse water for days. He wouldn't give up, for he was driven by his intuition—and he was right. The first indication was a marker, a stele covered with strange glyphs. Then the unnatural sudden small rise that could have been a hillock, but wasn't. Underneath the rank growth, the strange trees that grew parallel to the ground, was a man-made pyramid of massive stones that had been cut and placed ages ago. It would take him years to clear the site.

He called it "Lubaantun," City of Fallen Stones. There would be no rich treasures like the finds at Chichen Itza, Mexico; no wonderful jewels like those found in Tomb 7 at Monte Alban. What was discovered there, however, would prove to be infinitely more awe-inspiring and mystical. Not even the finds in the pyramids of Egypt could compare to this unique, undatable artifact.

The year was 1924, the place British Honduras, now called Belize. F. A. Mitchell-Hedges would present to the world an incredible and unique artifact, a quartz crystal carved in the shape of a human skull. He was an adventurer, a man of action, with a zest for exploration. His motto: "Follow your star, even if your star proves to be a false guide, even if you leave behind no material treasures, you will have riches in the hearts of those who have drawn strength from your strength" (from *Danger My Ally*, his autobiography). Mitchell-Hedges was also an author and soldier of fortune whose listing in *Who's Who in Great Britain* is longer than that of Sir Winston Churchill.

This exciting outlook on life must also have been shared by Lady Richmond-Brown, his companion and possible financier on the expedition. In her early 30s, she had been told she had only six months to live. She asked to accompany Mitchell-Hedges, saying: "I want to die with a thrill." Perhaps she thrived on the adventure, for she lived to be 63! Lady Richmond-Brown wrote a book about the trip entitled *Unknown Tribes, Uncharted Seas*.

No other artifacts comparable to the Crystal Skull were found at Lubaantun by this or any other archaeological expedition, at least nothing that displayed such sophisticated artistry or advanced knowledge of anatomy. Much to everyone's disappointment, there was (and unfortunately still is) no way of knowing where the Crystal Skull originated.

Anna's Discovery

F.A. Mitchell-Hedges' adopted daughter, Anna Le Guillon Mitchell-Hedges, often accompanied her famous father on his travels. Sixteen years old at the time, she was with him in British Honduras for this hot and sometimes frustrating dig.

Anna, nicknamed "Sammy," spied a shiny,

F.A. Mitchell-Hedges, Lady Richmond Brown and Dr. Thomas Gann on Lubaantun Expedition in 1920s.

glittering object under the earth. It was just out of reach, under the walls of the ruins of the ancient Mayan temple. Earthquakes had toppled the wall, and there was much debris strewn about. Remembering the admonition to not touch any artifact found until it was either photographed or painstakingly plotted and charted carefully on paper, she refrained from any attempt to retrieve it herself.

It was with great difficulty that the workers removed the giant rock slabs that made up the temple walls, and it was on Anna's 17th birthday that the last stone was reverently removed, freeing the captivating shiny object—a clear crystal skull—from its resting place in the earth.

The local Maya natives went wild with joy when they saw the unearthed artifact, and began dancing excitedly around the Skull and paying homage to it by bowing before this sacred relic. It seemed as if they recognized it. They immediately erected an altar to support the Skull for their worship.

Their excitement was great and they insisted on celebrating for the next several days. Mitchell-Hedges was in a quandary not knowing how he could persuade them to return to work, so he offered to give the priceless artifact to the Chief of the natives if they would only return to their excavating. The natives readily agreed, and by the next day they were obediently back at work.

It would be several months later before the

Anna Mitchell-Hedges and Crystal Skull in 1987.

Photo: *Mark Chorvinsky/Strange Magazaine*

detached lower jaw was found nearby. It too was in perfect condition, and only then did the full impact of this incredible find hit Mitchell-Hedges.

He was as puzzled as the other members of the expedition. Who made this unbelievable Skull? Were the Mayans actually capable of such a high degree of skill? He was really looking for Atlantis, thinking he might find some clues in British Honduras. Was this then a long-lost artifact from Atlantis? He never found out, although he had the Skull in his possession for the rest of his life.

Three years later when the expedition was ready to return to civilization, the Maya people gave the Crystal Skull back to Mitchell-Hedges in a noble show of gratitude for all the benefits they had received as a result of this expedition—income from jobs, tools and utensils, medical attention, and other modern lifesaving conveniences.

The Skull had been buried for untold ages. Now that it was unearthed and brought into contact with modern civilization, it would captivate the world once again.

Archaeology in the Last Century

At the time of Mitchell-Hedges' discovery of Lubaantun, French and English explorations had been going on in Central America for over a hundred years. However, archaeological exploration was not always profitable.

17th February, 1968

Mr. F N Dorland,
Messrs Dorlands,
280 Panoramic Highway,
Mill Valley.
California. 94943

The Rock Crystal Skull first appeared during our expedition to Lubaantum in 1926. We went during 1926, and left before the rainy season in 1927.

We found the building, and were digging in the temple, moving a heavy wall which had fallen on the altar. This took some time because the rocks were so heavy we could only move about 6 a day and left completely exhausted.

I came upon the Skull buried beneath the altar, but it was some three months later before the jaw was found which was about 25 feet away.

On this expedition ws:

Father   (dec)
Myself
Jane Houlson (dec) Father's secretary.
Capt. Joyce (dec) British Museum
Dr. Gann
Lady Richmond Brown (dec)

A. Mitchell-Hedges

(sgd)

This is a letter of authenticity from Anna Mitchell-Hedges to Frank Dorland explaining about the Crystal Skull's discovery in Lubaantun.

For example, Lord Kingsborough, who financed expeditions, was one of the greatest collectors of manuscripts, but he died in debtors' prison, unable to pay the bills of his paper supplier for one of the books he published on Central America.

American adventurer Edward H. Thompson fared better. He explored the Yucatan for nearly 50 years, from 1885 until his death in 1935. He discovered the Sacred Well at Chichen Itza (where ruins of an ancient Mayan city are located). He took up deep-sea diving in order to explore it, and along with a Greek pearl diver, recovered its treasures.

His greatest contribution, however, may well have been that he was the first to take Bishop de Landa's stories of the myths and legends of the Maya seriously, and his discoveries were proof they were based on fact. (The Bishop de Landa was the Bishop of Yucatan in the 1500s. In 1566, he had every Mayan document he could find destroyed, believing them to be the work of Satan.)

In the 18th and 19th centuries in England, the term *archaeology* had a very different meaning from the accepted use of the word today in America. Originally spelled *archaiology*, it was defined as "ancient history generally."

In the 1920s and '30s, the United Kingdom gave their explorers grants, and it was the policy to take everything in a concession home to England. Even so, the British government was not overly generous with funds. Usually the books an explorer wrote of his adventures were the major source of income (as were the five books Mitchell-Hedges wrote on his travels).

It has been said that artifacts were considered the personal finds of the explorer, and under a true gentlemen's agreement, no visiting archaeologist would write about another's finds. Perhaps that explains why Dr. Thomas Gann, the medical officer of British Honduras who accompanied Mitchell-Hedges at Lubaantun, never mentioned the Crystal Skull in his writings. He probably considered it to be the dig of Mitchell-Hedges and only wrote of his own experiences. (Dr. Gann, along with J. Eric Thompson, wrote a book of his explorations entitled *The History of the Maya*.)

Mitchell-Hedges contributed extensively to museums from all of his expeditions. Numerous items went to the British Museum and to the Museum of the American Indian (Heye Foundation) in New York City.

Lubaantun

Lubaantun, one of the last great Mayan centers built around the 8th or 9th century A.D., was situated on extremely fertile soil. The area is liana-covered and heavy with vegetation. It was apparently a trade center for the cacao bean (which is used to make chocolate). The city covered an area of over seven and a half acres. There were pyramids over 40 feet tall, but the

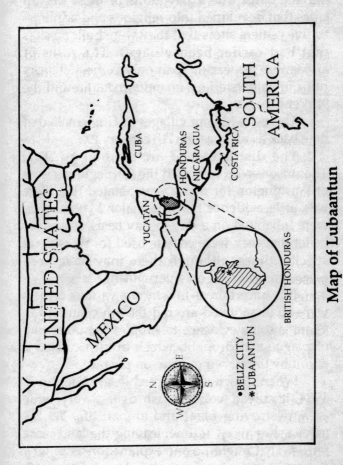

Map of Lubaantun

most spectacular part of Lubaantun was its huge amphitheater, one of the largest found in all the Mayan ruins. The excavations of most Mayan cities that developed into religious and administrative centers show that they were built on sites that had earlier been villages. The ruins of Lubaantun appear to span only some 150 years prior to its mysterious abandonment around the 9th century A.D.

There are Mayan villages in Guatemala that date back as early as the 7th century B.C.

The distinguished archaeologist J. Eric Thompson, who was with the Carnegie Institute of Washington for many years, stated that there was little evidence that the major Mayan ruins were inhabited on a day-to-day basis. It was his belief that they were centers used for worship at specific times, although there may have been priests in residence on a permanent basis.

It is uncertain as to why the various centers were all abandoned around the 9th century A.D. There is some evidence to support the possibility of plague and drought, which in turn caused a revolt by the starving common people.

When Chochonal erupted in the Yucatan in 1984, it spread volcanic ash over a very wide area, destroying plant and animal life. Yet the ash washes away in time, leaving the land more fertile. That might be one explanation as to why the ceremonial sites were abandoned. Other evidence indicates that they were merely moved.

The mapping of Lubaantun was done in

1970 by an expedition sponsored by the University of Cambridge, University of Harvard, and the Peabody Museum. This expedition and others later in the decade proved Lubaantun was a planned city. It did not grow along the lines of topography, but at one point was extended by means of containment walls. The walls held an excess of 3,000 cubic meters of rubble for foundations.

The head of the expedition, Dr. Norman Hammond, stated that the excavators were surprised by their discovery that Lubaantun was occupied for such a short period of time and during a very recent period of history. He offered one possible explanation. About the time Lubaantun was settled, Pusilha, which was 30 miles to the southwest along a natural trade route, apparently ceased to function as a ceremonial center, though it was continued as a settlement.

Discovered in the 1920s, Pusilha was visited by Dr. Eric Thompson, who observed a large number of inscribed stelae. The dates showed that these monuments were erected in 573 A.D. and 731 A.D.

Dr. Hammond cites another incident to support this theory: In Guatemala, a religious center was moved more than twice the distance of that between Pusilha and Lubaantun in the later part of the eighth century A.D. That move, from Alter de Sacrificio's to Seibal, apparently took place due to political pressure from an expanding Mayan state farther down the Usumacita river system. But no evidence of a similar process was established for Lubaantun, and the building of such a large center and its abandonment a century and a half later remains one of the many unsolved mysteries.

A more startling explanation is offered by Jose Arguelles, Ph.D. In his book, *The Mayan Factor: Path Beyond Technology,* he states:

"The Mayan Great Cycle is actually the description of a galactic beam measuring 5200 tuns, or 5125 earth years in diameter. The earth entered such a beam August 13, 3113 B.C., and will leave it in the year 2012 A.D. The purpose of the electromagnetically charged beam is to accelerate the evolved DNA into a technology-extruding organism that creates in effect a planetary exo-nervous system. When the exo-nervous system is in place, acceleration becomes exponential and phases into synchronization.

"Acceleration is measured by the collapse in the time it takes one human to communicate to another from halfway around the globe. Once maximum acceleration is achieved, when communication is electronic and virtually instantaneous, then it becomes synchronization: the equally exponential rate of linking up every single human organism with each other through utilization of the planetary exo-nervous system, thus creating a sensitive aggregate operating as a unified, planetary consciousness. Once maximum synchronization is attained, the exo-nervous system will fall away, being replaced by the more efficient medium of telepathic synchronicity. The planet will then be initiated into the Galactic Federation.

"August 16-18, 1987 [the important date on which the Harmonic Convergence took place] marks the point at which the galactic beam phases from acceleration to synchronization, while December 21, 2012 is the date of galactic synchronization.

"The purpose of the classic Maya was to synchronize the terrestrial calendar cycle with the galactic acceleration beam. Once done, they left, leaving the precise calendar and the knowledge transmitted by seers and symbols cloaked in the garb of myth, the prophecy of the return of Quetzalcoatl. The return is set for August 16, 1987."

Note that millions of people throughout the world joined in meditations for peace on our planet that day. (See Chapter 7 for further information on the Mexican deity Quetzalcoatl.)

At Altun Ha, 30 miles north of Belize City, David M. Pendergast, the archaeologist in charge of the excavations in the 1960s for the Royal Museum of Ontario, Canada, states: "Tombs within the site center were major structures, and the crude form of tomb construction encountered in the tombs lying outside the site

2-12   MARCH 10 1935   NEW YORK AMERICAN—A Paper for People

Atlantis Was No Myth but the Cradle Of American Races, Declares Hedges

AMAZING—Explorer Hedges (right) examining some astounding discoveries in the "Cradle of Civilization," he mina heads reduced to his size. Left, petrified stone head, once the wooden top of Christ-stick with skull showing same formation as that of the American Indian.

Excavations of Twenty-one Sites on Five Caribbean Islands Confirm His Theory of Pre-Flood Cataclysm, Says Noted Explorer

By F. A. MITCHELL-HEDGES,
Famous Explorer, F.R.G.S., F.R.S.A., F.R.S.
F.R.A.I., F.L.S., Member of the Maya
Committee of the British Museum

MANY weirdly strange mysteries are explained by discovery of evidences of the world's oldest known culture —a pre-Flood civilization—in the Bay Islands, off the coast of Honduras.

The most isolated primitive Indian tribes I have lived among twenty—retain ancient rituals from some dim past.

A "Feast to the God of Fertility" it is the Old World "Harvest Festival." A "wailing ceremony" for the dead: here we

American Races Born in Atlantis

Archaeological Finds at Lubaantun

center was characteristic of all priestly interments at Altun Ha."

This may help explain why no major artifacts were recovered at Lubaantun, for nothing was found that exhibited the high degree of technical skill embodied in the Crystal Skull. The site was cleared, but deep excavation of the surrounding area was not done. Four figurines, in a group of twelve found, showed distinct Oriental/Mongoloid features. Racial characteristics of all races—Negroid, Asian and Caucasian, with and without beards—are found in the portrait-type pottery of pre-Columbian America. This would seem to indicate a world trade contact.

A. Von Wuthenau (author of *Unexpected Faces in Ancient America*), a specialist in pre-Columbian art at the University of the Americas in Mexico City, tentatively dated his latest find as 2500 years old. According to the Boston Sunday Globe (November 10, 1985), it is a terra cotta model of an ancient sailing ship manned by figurines of ten oarsmen, all with striking Japanese features. The model is one foot long; the oarsmen, two inches high. It was discovered at a burial site in the Guerrero region of Mexico.

It is believed that there was a regular trade route all through Mexico up into California. Turquoise from the Santa Fe, New Mexico area has been found in burial sites in the Yucatan. Large pieces of crystal are found in Calaveras County in California. Interestingly enough, the

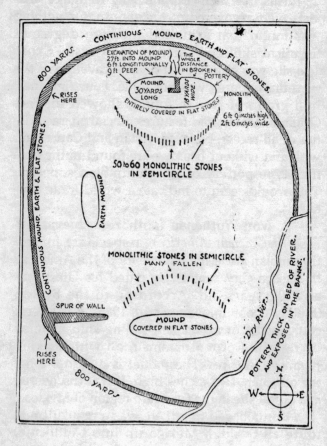

Site of Lubaantun

Spanish word for skull is *calaveras*. California crystal contains vermicular inclusions identical to those observed in the Mitchell-Hedges Crystal Skull. This poses the possibility that the Crystal Skull may have been carved from quartz crystal found in California.

So we see that this civilization was extremely advanced, and probably had extensive trade routes extending in many directions for long distances. The Mayan civilization reached its zenith between 300 A.D. and 900 A.D. Then, for reasons not understood, this unique civilization collapsed and its people mysteriously disappeared or migrated elsewhere.

F.A. Mitchell-Hedges' Association with Skull

Sensationalism was the keynote in journalism in the first quarter of the 20th century. Mitchell-Hedges, for years a correspondent for the London Times, exploited this to the fullest. He wrote of strange creatures, enormous fish, lost civilizations, unknown tribes, but he did not write about the Crystal Skull. The articles that began to appear in the '30s and '40s were written by newspeople.

In his autobiography, *Danger My Ally*, published in London, a chapter titled "The Skull of Doom and a Bomb" leads off with a full-page picture of the Crystal Skull. Other than the caption there were only 13 lines of type regarding the Skull itself.

"We took with us (to Africa in 1948) also the

sinister Skull of Doom of which much has been written. How it came into my possession, I have reason for not revealing. The Skull of Doom is made of pure rock quartz crystal, and according to scientists it must have taken 150 years, generation after generation, working all the days of their lives, patiently rubbing down with sand an immense block of rock crystal until the perfect skull emerged. It is at least 3,600 years old, and according to legend was used by the High Priest of the Maya when performing esoteric rites. It is said that when he willed death with the help of the skull, death invariably followed. It has been described as the embodiment of all evil. I do not wish to try to explain this phenomena."

When the book was published in the United States by Little, Brown and Co. in 1958, all reference to the Crystal Skull was deleted.

Why? The editors at both publishing houses had no comment to make. The Crystal Skull had received wide publicity in the London press, which would presumably create interest and increase sales of the book. Ordinarily publishers are eager to take advantage of any available publicity.

At any rate, it is doubtful that Mitchell-Hedges saw the Skull as evil, in spite of his comments, but he did have a flair for the dramatic. He was very aware that it was powerful. Except for the time he left it as security for a loan to finance another expedition, he kept it in his personal possession at all times for the rest of his life.

Chapter Three

SCIENTIFIC INVESTIGATION

The first scientific investigation of the Crystal Skull began in 1964 when Anna Mitchell-Hedges brought the Skull to the Dorlands in New York City. Frank Dorland and his wife, Mabel, were internationally known art conservators.

They had first heard of the Crystal Skull from a neighbor, Francis Fowler III, who owned the Southern Comfort distillery. (Interestingly, his hobby was buying famous drinking cups for the distillery, and in his collection was one once owned by Rasputin, the famous Russian monk.) Fowler was already acquainted with F. A. Mitchell-Hedges, having previously purchased some items from this unique world traveler. At that time, Mitchell-Hedges had for sale a very rare icon (holy picture).

Subsequently, the Dorlands authenticated this icon as the Black Virgin of Kazan Icon, one of the greatest of all Christian relics from Russia.

Frank Dorland was uniquely qualified to study the Crystal Skull. One of the foremost art conservators in the United States, he was for many years conservation consultant to many museums and cultural institutes. At the time, his private conservation laboratories were acknowledged to be the finest in the western United States.

Early in his career, he pioneered and developed a special artist's wax for restoration, conservation, and for use in either hot or cold wax techniques for painting. It was the first scientifically developed art wax in the history of art. (Known as Dorland's Wax Medium, it is produced by Siphon Arts, San Rafael, CA).

Dorland came to the work of art restoration in a traditional way. His grandfather Abbott was a photographer and restorer of art in the Midwest. Presently, less than half a dozen universities offer art conservator courses, and when Dorland began, there were none.

In the field of restoration, the first step in treating any painting (or any other valuable art object) is to make a complete, microscopically detailed examination and analysis. This includes visual and photo examinations using polarized, infrared and ultraviolet light sources. X-ray examination is included whenever indicated. Dorland is a master of control in photographic techniques and analysis. Only after the examination is complete and procedures recommended are the contracts negotiated and all records filed.

These techniques and knowledge would be put to good use in the study and authentication of the Crystal Skull.

Though Frank and Mabel had known each other since junior high school, they were not married until after Frank had attended the university for six years. Immediately after the wedding they opened their first art studio in the historic Casa de Bandini in Old Town San Diego.

World War II interrupted this endeavor, and Frank spent most of the war years as an artist in the engineering preliminary design department of Consolidated Aircraft Corporation, at Lindbergh Field in San Diego, California. (He did the original renditions of such aircraft as the Catalina Patrol plane and the B-24 Liberator Bomber, as well as others.)

After World War II, the Dorlands built a studio in the hills above La Jolla, California, and resumed their joint career in the art field. He and Mabel subsequently joined the International Institute for the Conservation of Museum Objects in London, England.

They continued their studies in the art fields. Because much of art is based on strong religious beliefs and often has magical symbolism and mysticism within it, they began a study of comparative religions. These studies led them all over the United States.

Early in their career, their reputation for excellence brought them into contact with many prominent people in the art field.

One in particular was Miss Amy Putnam. Choosing to remain anonymous, she was one of the main supporters of the San Diego Art Museum in Balboa Park. She lived nearby in a mansion which was filled with art treasures. She had almost five hundred priceless Russian icons, some of which were stacked like cordwood in an upstairs closet!

She gave the Dorlands a contract to restore some of the more select ones. For several years they spent every Monday morning returning art work that had been freshly cleaned and varnished. They would then collect another selection of icons—crumbling, grimy specimens—to process and photograph. It would take them several months to restore each set of icons.

Their work on Miss Putnam's collection would make them a logical choice for the task of later authenticating the Black Virgin of Kazan Icon, owned by F.A. Mitchell-Hedges.

The Dorlands had been in touch with F.A. Mitchell-Hedges and Anna Mitchell-Hedges since 1950. In 1959 Mitchell-Hedges died, leaving Anna in charge of their treasures—including the Crystal Skull and the Icon.

Later Anna sent the Icon to the Dorlands in San Francisco, where it cleared customs in 1962. In 1964 Anna brought the Icon to New York City at the close of the first half of the World's Fair, where the Icon was put on display.

After consultations with the Dorlands at the

Black Virgin of Kazan Russian Icon and Crystal Skull

Icon Pavilion on the fairgrounds, the Museum of the American Indian, and later at her hotel room, Anna Mitchell-Hedges decided that the Dorlands should take both the Skull and the Icon back to their San Francisco headquarters.

The day they left New York, a World's Fair police armoured limousine took the Dorlands, Ms. Mitchell-Hedges, the Icon, and the Crystal Skull to the plane, where Ms. Mitchell-Hedges patiently waited until the plane departed with the Dorlands and her precious, irreplaceable treasures. The Crystal Skull even had its own seat booked!

The Black Virgin of Kazan Icon

The Black Virgin of Kazan Icon is the Miracle Icon representing the Holy Mother of Russia. This amazing artifact has a unique history also.

Its power reportedly drove the Poles out of the Kremlin in their losing battle with the Russians. The Cathedral of Kazan was built inside the walls of the Kremlin in commemoration of this event. Later, the Cathedral was torn down by the Bolsheviks, who believe that God does not exist. The ground where the Cathedral once stood is still vacant. Reportedly, no building will stand there. When workers attempt to build on that exact spot, the walls mysteriously fall down.

The Icon depicts the hope and the salvation of the Mysterious Mother who nourishes and strengthens and provides for all who come to her.

Interestingly, the analysis of the pigments used in painting the Icon indicated to the Dorlands a process used before the 14th century. This confirmed that the Icon is undoubtedly the one recorded as being a coveted possession of the Old Kazan Monastery since 1579. It was probably painted in the 12th or 13th century.

White Russians tell of its miraculous powers that forced Napoleon to retreat from the gates of Moscow, and its power to heal the blind. Some also believe it will be instrumental in toppling the Communist regime. The protective riza that surrounds the Icon is encrusted with 158 matched rubies, 32 huge emeralds in a halo, six large sapphires, 150 baroque and other pearls, and 663 diamonds—including one large cinnamon diamond (placed between the letters OH in the halo around the head of the infant Jesus).

Smuggled from Russia during the time of the Revolution, it remained hidden in Poland until 1935. Mitchell-Hedges purchased it in 1953.

Authentication of the Crystal Skull

Dorland became greatly intrigued with the Crystal Skull. The Black Virgin was something he could study and ultimately verify as authentic. It fitted perfectly with his specialty and presented no unusual problems. But the Crystal Skull was a different kind of challenge. It could be photographed, but not analyzed. It did not fit any of the patterns of other great works of art. There was no legend, no myth, no record, no reference to go on.

The Dorlands had possession of the Crystal Skull for over six years. At first, Dorland did not find anything particularly unusual about the physical makeup of it.

Due to its great monetary value, it was always kept in a Mill Valley, California bank vault when it was not being subjected to study. One night, having worked too late to return it to the vault, Dorland was relaxing in front of the fireplace, with the Skull on the coffee table in front of him. He realized that the eyes of the Skull were reflecting the fire exactly. This unique (accidental?) viewing led to the discovery of the mysterious and unique optical properties cleverly carved into the Skull.

Underneath his microscope, Dorland began to discover incredible optics of a very sophisticated nature. Halfway back in the roof of the mouth of the Skull there is a broad, flat plane similar to a 45 degree prism. This surface can direct light from beneath the Skull into the eye sockets.

If the Skull were placed on a stone altar having a concealed interior firebox and a light hole up through the stone to where the Skull was sitting, the flickering flames could be reproduced visually as being alive in the eye sockets. There is also a thin ribbon-like surface carved next to this flat plane that could act as a magnifying

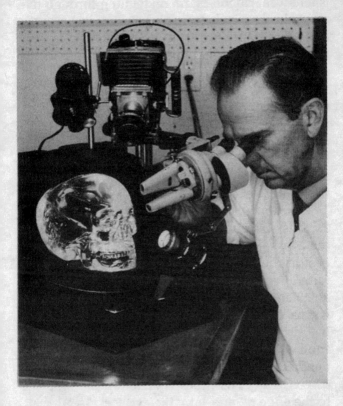

Frank Dorland examining Crystal Skull through binocular microscope. Microscopic studies of surface scratches and grinding marks reveal the Skull underwent at least three major changes—probably by three distinct and separate civilizations.

reading glass. Next to the 45 degree prism there is a natural ribbon prism. Extending through the more than six inches of solid rock quartz crystal, this channel is free from veils and inclusions. Print viewed through this is not only legible, but also undistorted and only slightly magnified.

Behind the intentionally carved prism, there is a concave and convex surface that acts as a light gatherer to bounce the light to the 45 degree prism and out to the eye sockets. The back of the Skull is formed as a beautiful camera lens, gathering light anywhere from the rear and reflecting it into the eye sockets.

Probably the most unusual aspect of the Skull is sharply illustrated in the delineation of the zygomatic arches. They are carved in relief, beside the cheekbones, just as they would be found in a human skull. This is not duplicated in any statue anywhere in the known world. There is a narrow channel from which enough material has been removed to have an air space. Light from either the back of the Skull or from underneath it will flow through these arches.

They act as pipes channeling the light up to the edge of, and into, the eye sockets. At their end there is a hollow depression, which acts as a lens and scatters light into the sockets. From this system, a light to the rear would show the same as a light underneath. Interruption of this light, such as a movement of a person behind it, would create an astounding optical effect.

Two bearing sockets or holes, which are

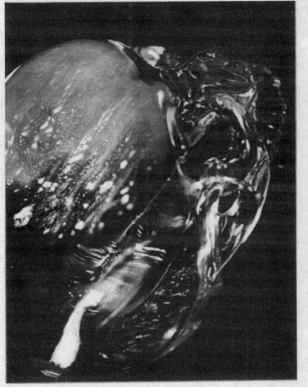

Crystal Skull showing zygomatic arches.

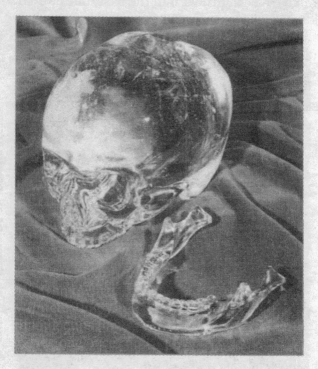

Crystal Skull showing detached jawbone.

invisible when the Skull is in an upright position, have been drilled into the base, one at each side. When two supporting axles or pivots are put in the holes, the Skull comes close to a balancing point and can be moved and rocked back and forth.

The jawbone, which is detached and removable, fits perfectly into two polished sockets and can be made to move up and down. The top surface of the cranium is slightly uneven. To the touch, it evidences much the same unevenness that a human baby's head does. The eye sockets vary and are slightly offset as would be the case in a human skull. With the exception of no suture marks on the top, it is as perfect as an anatomical scientific model.

How Was the Skull Made?

The actual handcrafting of quartz crystal art objects can be explained, for the crystalline structure of rock quartz crystal allows it, with a light touch and a gentle tap, to be shaped into the most delicate and exotic shapes.

Chinese, Japanese, Mongolian, Amerindian and pre-Columbian Meso-American cultures have all known this method for producing exquisite art. Water is used with rock and abrasive sand for polishing. However, that does *not* explain the technical knowledge of the prisms and reflected light. It is possible that the art of prism grinding was known, then became a lost art.

For example, a concave ground obsidian

lens was brought up from the sea bottom at Esmeraldas, Ecuador, and miniscule concave mirrors ground by an unknown process, which may have been used for magnification, have been unearthed at La Venta, Mexico. (La Venta is from the Olmec civilization, as is San Lorenzo, Mexico. San Lorenzo was occupied by the Olmec from 1200 B.C. to 900 B.C.)

Hewlett-Packard Investigation

In December of 1970, Dorland took the Crystal Skull to the Hewlett-Packard Laboratories in Santa Clara, California for testing. This laboratory is a world leader in electronics, computers, etc. They are experts in electronic quartz technology, probably one of the best. They also produce the precision quartz crystals used in the Hewlett-Packard oscillators and quartz crystal thermometers. The lab procures raw electronic crystal and then precisely cuts and shapes it into electronic oscillators (gold-plated quartz crystal wafers that vibrate at a precise frequency).

The lab performed two significant tests on the Crystal Skull. Submerging it in a bath of index-matching benzyl alcohol and viewing it under a polarized light, they determined that it had been cut without regard to the axis and that it was a single crystal. The orientation of the X-Y axis and the "veils" revealed by the polarized light showed that the jawbone, now a completely separate piece, had originally come from the same piece of crystal. The people at

Hewlett-Packard Investigation of Crystal Skull showing immersion tank with Skull in it (barely visible).

Hewlett-Packard stated that the size and clarity of the crystal alone made it a rarity. One worker said, "There is no way of proving its age. A lot of the ideas of mystery and evil that have sprung up around it could easily have come from the eyes. By shifting the light source or moving the angle of view even slightly, an infinite variety of refraction patterns can be seen. They could be quite hypnotic."

There, as elsewhere, the Crystal Skull created a stir of excitement. Even among people familiar with crystal and its properties, it raised as many questions as were answered. The exquisite workmanship and high gloss of the finish cause it to appear brand new, but it was the consensus of the lab experts that, given a crystal of the same size, these foremost producers of crystal components in the world today could not possibly produce a skull of comparable quality.

History of Lapidary

Experts agree that from samples, drawings and stone engravings found in ancient tombs, the art of lapidary (cutting, polishing and engraving precious stones) has existed at least since 5000 B.C., or for 7000 years. There is reason to believe that this is a conservative date.

The existing examples of carved stones are of turquoise, lapis lazuli, amethyst and crystal, jade, and more rarely, rubies. Lapidary tools wear out very quickly, literally being "used up," and there is little to indicate what the most ancient ones were made of. However, by 3000 B.C. very fine jewel-bearing machinery was in use. Though the knowledge was subsequently lost, there was also a visual magnification aid of some type then in use. Examples of unquestioned antiquity bear such tiny intricate details that can only be appreciated today under a magnifying glass. A knowledge of optics was a prerequisite for the engraving work done on many ancient artifacts.

The best cutting tool employed by the ancients was sapphire. A slurry of sand was also in use throughout the world, especially in cutting slabs of granite and marble. Using a string or rope or metal rod, and sawing back and forth as a slurry of sand and water is dribbled on, a groove will be quickly cut. This basic process is still in use today for marble, onyx and granite, but power machinery is employed and silicone carbide and water has replaced the use of sand and water.

In China today, one classic method still used to cut and polish jade is a foot-powered machine. The operator pedals, as one would a bicycle, to revolve a shaft that accommodates a variety of small tools, either of metal or stone. Here again, a "mud" of sand and water or pulverized crystal and water is used as an abrasive. This method was in use in ancient times in Tibet, Mongolia, India, Egypt and Babylon.

When canned food became available in the early 1900s, the top of the tin can was utilized by lapidaries. Put on a revolving shaft and used as a saw, the metal carrying the sand or abrasive slurry would cut very thin ridges.

Ancient Crystal Carving Techniques

The early cutting of crystal was accomplished mainly by chipping the crystal into the desired shape. The chips would then be pulverized and used for further grinding and polishing. Crystal, because its structure is similar to flint, can be shaped by using a small hammer to chip it. Very intricate designs can be formed in crystal with proper skill.

Although no one can say with absolute certainty *how* the Skull was made, one likely theory maintains that the Crystal Skull was formed and carved by rotary grinding, chipping, and hand rubbing. The entire face area was roughed out by chipping. The rough shaping of the eye sockets was by use of a rotary grinding device. The chipping of a piece of crystal places stress on the crystal itself. Immersed in a special refracting oil and viewed by polarized light, these stress marks show up as wavy lines.

It is possible to detect rotary tool marks under a binocular microscope, for modern machine tools leave marks that are repeated identically. The ancient hand rotary devices, like the patina on silver, leave scratches that go in every conceivable direction.

In early Greek and Roman times and in India, crystal was only shaped to remove the ofttimes ugly matrix. Very little shaping or smoothing was done, in order to save as much of the crystal as possible.

In the Middle Ages, crystal balls were made in Japan and China by first being hand-chipped into a rough ball, then by grinding and hand polishing. Unfortunately, 50 to 90 per cent of the crystal would be lost in this manner. Absolute control was required, only one delicate chip at a time was made, for an error would mean hours of work to rectify a mistake.

Dorland's Experiences with Quartz Crystal

When he began to work with quartz crystal, Dorland found that it would easily chip, crack or splinter. Though crystal is 7 on the scale of hardness, all crystals do not have the same characteristics. An experienced art conservator, Dorland had a good knowledge of gems and lapidary work. It seemed only logical to him that the crystal should be cut to achieve maximum size and minimum loss.

To solve the problem of flaking, he began to study the uncut pieces. He would immerse a piece in liquid, using benzyl alcohol. He would wet it with oil, or study it with sunlight coming through it.

Slowly, he began to learn that if he would *talk* to the crystal—asking what its best shape should be, how it should be cut—he would intuitively come to know how best to work with the inherent energies in the crystal, because his voice would activate these energy flows.

An understanding of the crystal's internal structure, how it could best be formed and shaped, would come to him. Following these energy flows, he found that he no longer had any problems in the cutting of crystal. No flaking, cracking or chipping occurred. It took time and practice, but his fingertips and eyes began to sense the energies in the crystal, how it could best be cut. When activated by voice and handling, the crystal oscillates in harmony with the human energies. It is a giving and a receiving of sensory vibrations, a type of psychometry. The resultant information produces beautiful, useful tools.

Conclusion

Dorland carefully examined the Crystal Skull for six years, subjecting it to every known scientific, nondestructive test. His conclusion (and that of other experts) was that even with the advanced technology we have today, it would be nearly impossible to carve as exquisite an object as the Mitchell-Hedges Crystal Skull.

Chapter Four

THE CRYSTAL SKULL PHENOMENA

In some mysterious manner that will one day have a scientific explanation, crystal, after being energized by a person, expands the individual's awareness beyond the five senses. The continuing association with the Crystal Skull began to have a mental effect on the Dorlands. During the years of their association and study of the Skull they neither smoked tobacco nor drank alcoholic beverages or coffee. They became vegetarians. The Crystal Skull began to express a definite personality to them. They began to be aware of the mental effect crystal was having on them.

Many other people have varying reactions to the Crystal Skull on seeing it for the first time also. Some become sleepy. Others have difficulty breathing, or their heart begins to pound.

In Dallas in 1986, the author Alice Bryant was very shaken both physically and mentally for nearly an hour after seeing the Skull again after nine years. It was a feeling akin to seeing someone who you have been very emotionally involved with but who has not been a part of your life for a long time. The strong rush of emotion, the memories of all the searching and studying, trying to understand the mystery of the Crystal Skull, came surging back. Her hands shook and she had difficulty getting her breath.

California friends of the Dorlands, visiting New York City, had written ahead to the Museum of the American Indian asking to see the Crystal Skull. They were told that it was not on display and would not be for some time. However, honoring their request, the Museum accommodated them with a private showing in the office of the secretary of the director. The secretary brought the Skull to them.

From the time Mitchell-Hedges had traveled with the Crystal Skull, it had been kept in a black wooden box, fitted with sponge rubber that had been made especially to fit it. The box had two doors that folded away from the back part, allowing the Skull to be viewed from the front and both sides, without being removed from the box. The secretary opened up the box for them so they could view it. The visitors were very interested in metaphysics and psychic phenomena, and they questioned the secretary at some length. She was adamant that all of it was a lot of nonsense and made it quite plain that they were taking up her valuable time and it would be best if they left. They thanked her for the opportunity of seeing the Skull.

She then replaced the cloth band with the buckles that went around the box, tightened them, and picked up the box to take it back to storage. She walked about halfway across the room and stopped dead in her tracks. She turned around and her face was drained of color. She was aghast. After a moment, when she could speak, she said, "It thumped me! Right through the cage, it thumped me!" She left then, extremely upset. No doubt she had moved hundreds of items from place to place in the museum. She had thought it ridiculous that people were placing any power in an art object. Yet, when she picked it up, the Crystal Skull "thumped" her.

Mr. Sibley Morrill, then editor of a major East Bay newspaper in Oakland, California, had an appointment to see the Crystal Skull while it was being studied at the Dorland home. He asked if he could bring a guest. When they arrived, it was discovered that Morrill's guest was the notorious Anton LaVey, then head of the Satanic Church in San Francisco.

Their combined viewing and discussion about the Skull continued on and on, until it was too late to return the Skull to the Mill Valley bank vault. That night after LaVey had departed, strong poltergeist effects took place. Strange noises were heard in the night, sounding like bouncing ping-pong balls. Kitchen utensils were strewn about, and a large plastic dialer on the phone was thrown across the room. Dorland got up to investigate, but found nothing. Due to the valuable paintings they frequently worked on as restorers, they had an unusually tight security system. Nothing was broken and no alarms set off, yet both the Dorlands heard the sound of a huge cat padding around, as though their house cat suddenly weighed 150 pounds. This experience convinced them to be more careful as to the type of person that should be allowed to visit the Crystal Skull!

On another occasion, a group of people visited the Crystal Skull one evening. The group included a psychiatrist, a minister, and a psychic. Having been carefully cleaned, the Skull was placed with a light illuminating it from below. All other lights were extinguished, and the group sat silently around the glowing art object. Even as they watched, the forehead of the Skull turned cloudy, then a milky white. A small darkish spot appeared on the side near the temple. The dark spot increased in size and intensity until it appeared that a major portion of the center mass of the Skull had simply dissolved and vanished. The outlines were still there, sharply visible, but the midsection of the solid rock quartz crystal had vanished. There was nothing to be seen. Nothing.

Later, over tea, discussion revealed that, with minor personal variations, each of the people in the room had seen the same thing.

Although the Skull is a perfectly colorless

piece of quartz crystal, on occasions it has appeared to change in color to shades of green, violet, purple, amber, red, and blue. At other times, the Crystal Skull has stimulated certain people's olfactory senses, giving the impression that it was emitting a distinctive musky odor which was impossible to describe, being both sweet and sour. A faint chorus of sounds resembling human voices and the sound of small silver bells have been heard by many people when in the presence of the Skull.

Frank Dorland once observed a halo around the Crystal Skull similar to the ring around the moon. It extended out about 18 inches and lasted approximately six minutes. "It made me want to be very, very still and very quiet," he stated.

As part of his ongoing scientific investigation, Dorland obtained a large authentic quartz crystal ball from the History Division of the Oakland, California Public Museum. After two years of proximity to the Crystal Skull, the crystal ball reproduced, to a lesser degree, some of the same phenomena: the sweet-sour odor and the visual effects. This was positive evidence that something physical was happening. The crystal did react to some unknown stimuli. It did change. It was not the result of one's imagination or wishful thinking, nor a hypnosis induced by the powerful form of the carving of the Crystal Skull. *Pure rock quartz crystal reacted to the energies around it!*

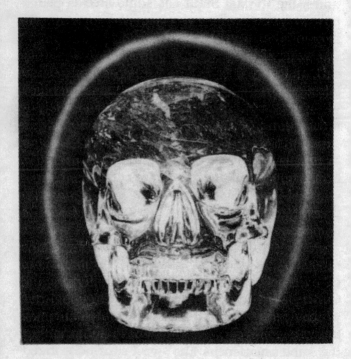

Crystal Skull showing recreated, simulated halo around it. This is how halo actually appeared during a meditation session.

As a result of his study of the Crystal Skull and a growing fascination with quartz crystal, Dorland began making crystal pendants, teardrops, crystal balls, and other unique hand working pieces as an adjunct to his studies of the Crystal Skull. (A hand working piece refers to a crystal object that has been fashioned to fit comfortably in one's hand. These pieces can be used for healing, meditation, divination, etc.)

The Dorlands began experimenting with the phenomena and energies emitted from quartz crystal. While meditating, they learned that quartz crystal acts not only as a receiver but also as an amplifier. Exactly why this alteration of consciousness works so well with crystal is not precisely understood, but many scientists and psychologists believe there is an energy interchange between certain portions of the brain and crystal. Thought waves are generated energy and they are very similar to radio waves. The brain may decode invisible frequencies to make an image the way a hologram decodes light rays to make a picture.

Neuroscientist Dr. Karl Pribam theorized that the brain receives sight in the form of a hologram and may decode invisible frequencies to make an image the way a hologram decodes light rays to make a picture. He speculates that the world as we perceive it may be a hologram that is translated by the brain into space and time. It is contact with that spaceless, timeless world of frequencies that provides us with super insight.

Crystals carved by Frank Dorland: Meditation Crystals, Handworking Pieces, and Healing Tools.

The Skull of Doom

Earlier in this century, the Crystal Skull had a much more sensational reputation. Much of this mysticism was fostered by Mitchell-Hedges in his autobiography, where he says: "It is stated in legend that [the Skull] was used by a high priest of the Maya to concentrate on and will death. It is said to be the embodiment of all evil. Several people who have cynically laughed at it have died, others have been stricken and become seriously ill."

After he wrote the above, there were incidents which occurred in several different places that seemed to reinforce this description of the Skull.

F.A. Mitchell-Hedges traveled with the Skull to many places. In Africa, it created a special stir. Following is a quote from a South African newspaper article in the 40s:

"The 'Skull of Doom,' a life-size skull fashioned from rock crystal more than 3,600 years ago and notorious for the bad luck it brings to those who view it, left another victim in its wake when it passed through East London in the Sterling Castle today in the possession of its owner, Mr. F.A. Mitchell-Hedges, the well-known explorer and ocean fisherman.

"Mr. Mitchell-Hedges will arrive in Durban tomorrow (Tuesday) on his way to Zululand.

"Within a few hours of photographing the Skull, Mr. Jack Ramsden, a newspaper cameraman, had the shock of his life when he started to make a print from the negative. As he switched on the apparatus there was a shattering explosion and the already darkened room was plunged into complete darkness.

" 'I ran from the room and nothing would take me back,' he told me a short time later. 'In my 20 years as a photographer I have never known this to happen to an enlarger.'

" 'They have flickered and gone out but I have never even heard of one exploding like this.'

"Mr. Mitchell-Hedges maintains that the Skull is the embodiment of all evil. It was used by the High Priest of the Maya civilisation before 1600 B.C. Legend says he took the Skull into the depths of the temple and concentrated on it, willing death.

"Death always came to someone connected with it."

The following is an excerpt taken from an English newspaper:

Explorer's Castle

"Mr. F.A. Mitchell-Hedges, millionaire British explorer and big game hunter whose name made news last year when he was reported lost in East Africa, has bought Farley Castle, between Wokingham and Reading, built in 1610 by the Gypsy King Simon the Red.

"Mr. Mitchell-Hedges' new abode will

house his collection of silver, said to be worth L500,000, and also the treasures he has collected in a lifetime of exploration and adventure in remote parts of the world.

"Among his collection is the 'Skull of Doom,' a life-sized rock crystal skull more than 3,600 years old, used by the High Priest of the ancient Maya civilisation as 'an instrument of death.'

"It is said to have a strange effect on people who look at it. Mrs. John Dixon Carr was taken ill after gazing at it for a few minutes; the same thing happened to Mrs. Arthur Conan Doyle."

Here is yet another excerpt from a newspaper cutting from the 1940s regarding the Skull:

Famous Explorer Buys Castle
by E.E.W.

"Legend says that the skull was the great religious object of the Maya which flourished in Central America thousands of years before the birth of Christ. Mr. Mitchell-Hedges discovered the ruins of the civilisation during his explorations in British Honduras.

"Asked whether he believed in the skull's evil influence Mr. Mitchell-Hedges said, 'I am not superstitious. I have an open mind, but some very queer things have certainly happened apparently in connection with it.'

"For example, the day he arrived in Zululand, the Royal House was struck by lightning, and he was warned by a member of Congress that it would be 'smelled out' by medicine men as it was considered to be more powerful than Stalin."

The warning letter referred to above reads as follows:

"Rome Farm"
Ixopo
25/10/49

Dear Mr. Mitchell-Hedges
   I am writing to let you know that your souvenir "The Skull of Doom" will be much sought after by the Zulu Sangu and will probably be stolen very soon.
   You will have read that members of the Zulu Royal House were struck by lightning—This will be associated with the return of "Zulu" by the so called medicine man—Zulu of I Zulu being lightning—your harmless souvenir will be smelt out as a valuable organising factor in native insurrection—in fact, it is from a native point of view more powerful than "Stalin".
   I am not interested one way or another in superstition, but can definitely say that I feel you must be careful, otherwise your trinkets can cause a very great deal of trouble in Africa.
   This thought occurred to me when replying

to a parson who felt that Members of his Black Flock, if able, should qualify as prime minister if fit—I stressed a fundamental difference and gave this "Skull of Doom" picture for his benefit —he was obviously worried and insisted that my observation had possibilities—Think that over.

I would be interested to hear from you, should you care to write at a future date.

Yours Sincerely,
Clifford M. Hulley

Frank Dorland says that a number of sensitives who have viewed the Skull have "perceived mysterious and evil visions emanating from the skull." He feels that the Skull has a fascinating attraction, even hypnotic. He stated, "I do not necessarily think it is an evil symbol, but I do feel it is trying to broadcast something, to communicate."

Present Reputation of the Crystal Skull
More recently, the Skull's reputation has improved a great deal. Most New Agers firmly believe that the Skull is here for a beneficent purpose, and that viewing it or touching it brings about positive feelings and changes to those who are near it.

Anna Mitchell-Hedges occasionally takes the Skull on lectures and exhibits it. She generously allows people to actually touch the Skull, and many even place their own personal crystals next to the Skull, supposedly to "charge" them.

One psychic, Lorraine Darr, who saw the Skull in Sedona, Arizona in 1987, had this to say about it: "When I laid my hands on it, I felt a hum, a buzz coming from it. There was a sense of energy that was nice. It felt like I was greeting an old friend." Some have reported these same kinds of energies emanating from the Skull when they have been near it.

Others who have spent time with the Skull feels it reaches them even *in absentia*. Catherine Bowman (author of *Crystal Awareness*, Llewellyn, 1987) has had unusual meditations regarding the Skull. She had seen the Skull on several occasions previous to an upsetting meditation near the Harmonic Convergence in August of 1987. Psychically gifted, she is able to easily tune into the Skull because it is so familiar to her. In this particular meditation, she saw the Skull with blood coming from it. It was a very upsetting experience, and she felt that perhaps it was a warning, and had to do with blood being shed in other parts of the world from needless warfare.

Dorland relates numerous incidents when scenes have miraculously appeared within the Skull. During a meditation with the Skull, he once witnessed thousands of people walking across a high mountain bridge from one village to another. On three different occasions a dark spot appeared which spread across one-half of the Skull and appeared to be a clear, black void surrounded by a band of very deep purple. Images of temples and skulls have appeared from time to time.

Whatever the reason for these phenomena, one thing can be agreed upon: they do indeed happen, and these strange visions and happenings cannot be discounted, for they have occurred to countless people throughout the world who have been in contact with the Skull at some point in their lives.

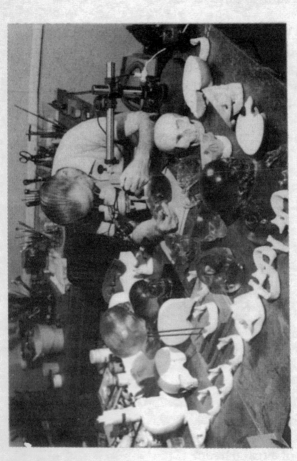

Dorland examining plaster cast and lucite scientific models of the Skull in his studio.

Chapter Five

FORENSIC RECONSTRUCTION

The Face of the Crystal Skull

Perhaps the most exciting event in the known history of the Crystal Skull occurred in 1986 when Francis Joseph courageously took the step so many had pondered. He had a likeness of the face made by forensic reconstruction.

A free lance writer on historical subjects both ancient and modern, Joseph first learned of the Crystal Skull while researching Lowland Maya for a project-investigation of Late Classic Maya society: studying the reason for its collapse and fate of its culture-bearers.

His father visited Anna Mitchell-Hedges in Ontario and was allowed to photograph the Skull. The startling realism of the crystal jewel convinced Joseph that it was not only a precious work of art, but a true-life rendering from the skull of a real person.

Proceeding on the assumption that the object represented a human prototype, a forensic reconstruction from its anatomical details would produce a likeness of who the model for the Crystal Skull was. If that could be done, it might be possible to ascertain the race of the original.

A reconstruction had never been attempted. Obviously it was out of the question to work on such a priceless artifact as the Skull itself, but the project began to enter the realm of possibilities when Anna Mitchell-Hedges put Francis Joseph in touch with Frank Dorland. Dorland agreed to allow Joseph to use the accurate plaster cast he had made to facilitate his own studies of the Crystal Skull.

Joseph states:

"I was aware that the expertise in forensic reconstruction—realizing in representational art vanished physiognomical characteristics from cranial remains—had reached high levels of accuracy in recent years, so much so that it is presently an accepted, important part in criminal investigation among police departments everywhere. But where does one find a qualified expert in forensic science? The Anthropology Department at Chicago's Field Museum referred me to Dr Clyde C. Snow, one of the leading physical anthropologists in the world today, most recently renowned for his investigation of the skeletal remains of Martin Bormann. Included in *American Men and Women of Science* since the early 1960s, Dr. Snow's association with the Forensic Science Foundation and the

American Academy of Forensic Science has been illustrious.

"I brought Mr. Dorland's plaster cast of the Crystal Skull to the Cook County Medical Examiner's office in Chicago, where Dr. Snow was able to examine it for the first time. Impressed by the general accuracy of its anatomical details, he was able to determine that it belonged to a woman in her late teens, short in stature, with possibly Amerindian features. The age range—from about 17 to 20 years—was determined by the degree of wear indicated on the last molars. The Skull, as an artwork, was not a composite of various skulls; the cranial elements were too closely related to each other not to belong to one female subject.

"But the cast also demonstrated significant anatomical errors, particularly in the incisors, which were clearly stylized. In the occlusal surface on the left side of the mandible, the first molar shows an X on the surface; in a human being, it should be marked instead with a plus (+) sign. Moreover, the suture marks which should be atop the dome are absent. In short, the Crystal Skull exhibited a very good overall medical likeness with some glaring errors in detail.

"While these detailed somatological errors argued against its mold-cast origins, they bespoke an extraordinarily high degree of portraiture on the part of its artist. Doubtless, it was the recreation of a real skull in quartz crystal. But how could so realistic a likeness be reproduced in so difficult a mineral? The artifact's general medical accuracy convinced some examiners that it had been cast from the mold of a human skull. But the Maya were not able to build the acetylene temperatures (*circa* 1723 degrees Centigrade) to liquify crystal. More importantly, once quartz crystal has been liquified and allowed to re-harden, it loses its crystalline chemical structure, which in the case of the M-H Skull, is still intact . . .

"After Dr. Snow's cursory examination, I wrote to Eugene Giles, the renowned professor of anthropology at the University of Illinois (Urbana) with my proposal. He recommended I contact Peggy C. Caldwell, consulting forensic anthropologist for the Office of the Chief Medical Examiner, in New York City. A collaborator at the Department of Anthropology in the Smithsonian Museum of Natural History, Dr. Caldwell is among America's leading researchers in human osteology, with membership in the American Association of Physical Anthropologists and the American Academy of Forensic Science (provisional). Her busy public appearance schedule includes lectures on Dental Anthropology, Facial Reproduction Techniques, Paleoanthropology in Action and the latest ideas in forensic science. With such a distinguished and appropriate background, Dr. Caldwell seemed ideally suited to restoring the Crystal Skull's lost face, and it was really with her that the artifact's reconstruction began.

"Responding enthusiastically to the request that she undertake the project, she sent me two case reports as recent examples of her work, one of which was a real-life sketch of Alexander the Great from a terra-cotta likeness. The high artistry and accuracy of the drawings were most impressive . . .

[At this time, Frank Dorland furnished Dr. Caldwell with a set of accurate scientific photographs of the Crystal Skull for reference. Caldwell said that the photos were extremely important, for between the photos and the plaster model, they could work with precision.]

"For hair reference, I sent her two reproductions of Mesoamerican hair styles (*The Ancient Maya*, S. Morely; *Everyday Life of the Aztecs*, Warwick Bray). One was an artist's rendering of Mayan women, the other a jadeite sculpture of Coatlicue, the Aztec mother-earth goddess in her role as the divine patroness of childbirth.

"Dr. Caldwell took the processed slide photographs of the plaster cast to Detective Frank J. Domingo (Composite Artist Unit, Latent Print Command, New York City Police Dept.) and the facial reproduction was under way."

Their procedure is described in Dr. Caldwell's own words:

"Our first step in preparing the sketch was to make scaled enlargement actual-size drawings of the cast. This was done by projecting my slide of the cast in the frontal view and moving and focusing the slide projector until the specimen label in the projected picture was exactly the same size as the specimen label in my possession. The features of the cast in the slide were then, consequently, actual size and were sketched in outline onto a plain piece of white, heavy bond paper. The same procedures were followed for creating an enlarged-to-real size outline of the cast in the left lateral view.

"Our next step was to add the outline of the facial soft tissue to the outline drawings of the cast. This was done using facial soft tissue thickness depth data for Southwest American Indians (Rhine, Unpublished, Personal Communication), which is the latest and only facial soft tissue thickness data for American Mongoloid populations that is available.

"The next step in preparing the two dimensional facial reproduction was to sketch in anatomical reference points for the facial details based on data from Caldwell (*The Relationship of the Details of the Human Face to the Skull and Its Application in Forensic Anthropology*. Master of Arts Thesis, Arizona State University, 1981). This step in the procedure was complicated by two factors. First there are no specific instructions available in the anthropological literature for the representation of the facial details in Mongoloid facial reproductions, with the exception of the epicanthic fold. Consequently, we had to use generalized anatomical reference points from the literature. Second, the Crystal Skull is itself an artistic representation of an individual's skull. This led to some difficulty and much discussion between Detective Domingo and myself concerning such features as the width of the nose, length of the nose, placement of the mouth, philtrum, etc. However, we resolved these difficulties by using what data that we could from the anthropological literature and mug-shot photographs of American/Indian/Mongoloid/Hispanic individuals from the Police Department Modus Operandi unit files. These photographs were selected of women fitting the general description of the individual represented by the Crystal Skull (Mongoloid in her twenties), and presenting the same sort of facial soft tissue outline and features, we sketched onto the two-dimensional facial reproduction. The photographs were selected to assist the artist in rendering the facial details and highlighting and/or shadowing the features to make the face appear as natural as possible.

"Once the facial outline and anatomical reference points for the facial details had been drawn onto the two-dimensional facial reproduction, Detective Domingo continued to work on the sketch, filling in the face.

"If this woman was indeed a member of the Mayan royalty, which Mr. Joseph has suggested, then the inclusion of earrings (a controversial point) would indeed make her look more 'regal' without detracting from the overall quality of the face.

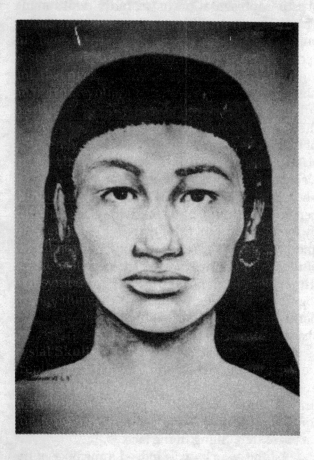

Forensic reconstruction showing face on the Crystal Skull.

"Miss Caldwell's initial reaction to the finished visage was: 'The completed two-dimensional facial reproduction at first struck me as looking far too "Oriental" in appearance, but, on thinking about it, it occurred to me that this female is presumed to be a representative of one of the earliest civilizations in Mesoamerican history; there is no reason to suppose that she shouldn't look more "Oriental" Mongoloid, rather than our modern ideal of the "American Indian" Mongoloid. Perhaps then, her appearance is more realistic than any of us had envisioned! Mr. Joseph commented that on a recent visit to several Central American countries, he noticed that many of the people he saw did indeed present more "Oriental" Mongoloid rather than straight "American Indian" Mongoloid features.'

"The pair of inconspicuous holes drilled at its center of gravity, together with its movable jaw, clearly define the Crystal Skull as a religious object. The skull was the particular emblem of the mother-earth goddess, the Aztecs' Coatlicue; Ixchel to the Maya. She was the foremost deity in the Mesoamerican pantheon, the personification of both creation and destruction . . . Given the high standing of the goddess and her grim trademark, the Crystal Skull's identification with Coatlicue-Ixchel seems likely.

"But what of the real woman who modeled for it? High priestess (the first priestess)? of the mother-earth cult or a victim (again the first)?

Through her sacrifice, in which she impersonated the goddess, the victim was believed to actually assume the identity of Mother Earth. It may have been that the real skull of this important lady was preserved and used until it began to deteriorate. If the priests then commissioned the likeness as a means of preservation, that might explain the disparity of accurate detail and anatomical errors. If the human prototype was no longer in perfect condition, some of its features, such as the front teeth, might have been so badly damaged they had to be stylized in the crystal duplicate. In any case, the Crystal Skull is a portrait of perhaps the most important person in Mesoamerican pre-history. Why else would the Mayas have selected this one skull to have been memorialized in so unique a manner?"

The excellent work of Ms. Caldwell and Detective Domingo has done justice to this most mysterious object. But the mystery is still unsolved. Who was the lady—high priestess or holy sacrifice?

Chapter Six

COMPARISON OF SKULLS

The Mitchell-Hedges Crystal Skull is a beautiful and mystifying artifact. It rarely evokes any feelings other than positive ones in the viewer. This is not necessarily the case when seeing the only other two authenticated life-size crystal skulls known to us at this time. In this chapter we will compare and contrast all of these unique crystal skulls.

Mitchell-Hedges Skull

It has been determined that this most perfectly formed of the skulls was carved from a single piece of unusually clear quartz crystal. It measures approximately 5 13/16 inches high by 7 7/8 inches long, and it is 4 29/32 inches wide. The M-H Skull weighs 11 pounds seven ounces. When viewed, it exhibits almost perfect bilateral symmetry. This object has been carved with total disregard for the axis of the crystal, which in itself represents a very high degree of technical workmanship, and even though it comes to us from uncharted antiquity, there are no traces of Metal Age workmanship. The Mitchell-Hedges Skull is considered to be nearly priceless. It *is* irreplaceable.

British Museum Skull

A second crystal skull resides in the British Museum of Mankind in London. There are marked similarities and marked differences between the two skulls. The one in the British Museum is less finished, less defined. The Mitchell-Hedges Skull shows great attention to the exact rendering of detail, a realism that goes far beyond art. Even its eye sockets are not identical, but are slightly off set as would be a normal person's eye sockets. It has the character of an anatomical study done in a scientific age.

The Mitchell-Hedges Skull has moving parts and its surface gleams with a strange interior luster, and it certainly is much more refined. The two skulls are also quite similar, however, and it is their similarity that raises some intriguing questions.

It is recorded that the skull in the British Museum was brought out of Mexico by a soldier of fortune during the reign of the Emperor Maximilian and his Empress Carlotta, but like its more finished relative, its origins too are shrouded in mystery. The caption on its register reads as follows:

"1898.1. Skull cut from a solid block of rock

crystal. Purchased from Tiffany's of New York. Brought from Mexico by a Spanish officer before the French occupation. In the possession of M.E. Boban of Paris and Mr. Sissons of New York. Nothing is known of its origin, etc." (The registration number 1898.1 is the date the specimen was obtained.)

Not much has been written about the British Museum skull, and for the most part it has been ignored by the Museum officials. It is kept in a locked case, with little testing allowed. For a period of time, this crystal skull was even taken out of view because of all the attention it attracted by hippies and flower children back in the 1960s who would come to the museum and station themselves around the skull. Apparently this kind of acclaim was embarrassing to officials at the Museum, and in 1967 the skull was removed from display by Dr. A.E. Werner, head of the museum's laboratory. Rumor spread that the skull was removed because it was discovered to be a fake!

The Mexican government has tried to have the skull returned to them, but have been unsuccessful in their efforts. They believe the skull is Mixtec in origin.

The first and most descriptive reference to the British Museum crystal skull was written by G.F. Kunz in *Gems and Precious Minerals*, published in New York in 1890:

"Rock crystal has not, in our time at least,

been discovered, in Mexico or Central America, of a quality or of sufficient quantity to be of much use to the arts, yet there have been found a number of interesting pre-historic objects made of rock crystal—skulls from 1 inch to 7 inches in width, crescents, beads, and other articles—of which the material is excellent, and the workmanship equal to anything done by the early lapidaries. Small skulls are in the Blake Collection at the United States National Museum, the Douglas Collection, New York, the British Museum, and the Trocadero Museum.

"A large skull, now in the possession of George H. Session of New York, is very remarkable . . . The eyes are deep hollows; the line separating the upper from the lower row of teeth has evidently been produced by a wheel made to revolve by a spring held in the hand, or possibly by a string stretched across a bow, and is very characteristic of Mexican work. Little is known of its history and nothing of its origin. It was brought from Mexico by a Spanish officer sometime before the French occupation of Mexico, and was sold to an English collector, at whose death it passed into the hands of E. Boban, of Paris, and then became the property of Mr. Session.

"That such large worked objects of rock crystal are not found in Mexico might lead one to infer its possible Chinese or Japanese origin. But it is evident that the workmanship of the skull is not Chinese or Japanese, or nature would have been more closely copied; and if the work were of European origin, it would undoubtedly have been more carefully finished in some minor details. Prof. Edward S. Morse of Salem, Mass., who resided in Japan for several years, and Tatui Baba of Japan, now of New York City, state positively that this skull is not of Japanese origin. Mr. Baba gives as one reason for his belief that the Japanese would never cut such an object as a skull from so precious a material.

"In ancient Mexico there was undoubtedly a veneration for skulls, for we find small skulls of rock crystal, notably the one in the Cristy Collection in the British Museum, incrusted with turquoise, and it may have been one of these that suggested the making of this skull, the one at the Trocadero Museum, and the smaller one. Two very interesting crescents are known, the one in the Trocadero Museum, the other in the collection of Dr. Maxwell Sommerville, in the Metropolitan Museum of Art, New York City. Beads of this material are sometimes found in the tombs with jadeite and other stone beads. They rarely have a diameter of an inch.

"Rock crystal in large masses has been reported from near Pachuca, Hidalgo, in the state of Michoacan, and in veins near La Paza in Lower (Baja) California; the center of the vein is said to be beautifully pellucid, but the sides are opaque white. It is not known whether the rock crystal used by the aborigines was obtained at a Mexican locality, or whether it came from

Calaveras County, Calif., where masses of rock crystal are found containing vermicular pro-cholorite inclusions identical with those observed in the large skull described above."

In the 20th century another look at the British Museum skull would be undertaken. A scientific comparison study of them done in 1936 for the anthropological magazine *Man* showed they were remarkably alike. The anthropologist involved in the study, Dr. G.M. Morant, conclud-ed they were copies of the same skull. Moreover, there were strong indications that this was a female skull! He concluded that they were from a common source.

In the British specimen, the orbits are unnaturally round, and no great attempt had been made to excavate the zygomatic arches or the bone which extends along the front or side of the skull beneath the orbit. In the Mitchell-Hedges Skull, these are well defined. Also, the Mitchell-Hedges Skull shows the definite shape of separate teeth while no attempt was made to realistically sculpture this in the British skull. Viewed as a whole, the Mitchell-Hedges Skull is vastly superior in finished details to the crude, rough configurations of the British specimen.

Frank Dorland feels that the British Museum skull is an unfinished "stand-in." If the jawbone were cut loose and other refinements made, the two would measure and look identical. Perhaps it was a first rough sketch by its creator, or an unfinished "spare" skull, used for whatever purpose it was fashioned.

Comparison of Physical Measurements

(Owing to the absence of sutures, only a few of the usual measurements can be taken accurately.)

Measurement	*British Skull*	*M-H Skull*
Glabellar-occipital length:	117 mm	174 mm
Maximum calvarial breadth:	135 mm	140 mm
Cephalic index:	76.3 mm	80.5 mm
Bizygomatic breadth:	117 mm	117 mm
Nasal breadth:	22 mm	24 mm
Breadth of left orbit:	34.5 mm	37.5 mm
Height of left orbit:	37 mm	33.5 mm
Left orbital index:	107.2 mm	89.3 mm

(Note that the difference in measurements is because the British skull is not fully carved out—it is an unfinished object.)

It is interesting to superimpose the outlines of both skulls. Trackings made from photographs show that the brain boxes diverge to an appreciable extent, but certainly no more than any two random skulls picked for examination. The orbits are not far apart, and Morant concludes that the outlines of the lower jaws, the teeth lines, and the nasal apertures are practically the same. The breadth at the zygomatic arches are identical, but the forms of the arches are slightly different. The close correspondence

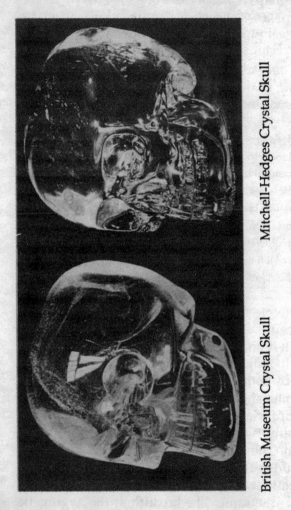

British Museum Crystal Skull   Mitchell-Hedges Crystal Skull

Comparison of Skulls

between the two outlines is remarkable.

According to Morant, this comparison makes it impossible to "avoid the conclusion that the crystal skulls are not of independent origin. It is almost inconceivable that two artificers, having no connection with one another, using different human skulls as models, should have produced specimens so closely similar in form as these two are."

Morant was of the opinion that they were representatives of the same skull, but that one might have been copied from the other. The only real difference between the two is that the British Museum skull is less detailed, less finished.

It would seem logical that of the two, the more finished would be the later specimen. Morant does not agree with this. He said, "Suppose that the British specimen was modeled from a human skull, and that at some later date the original crystal was copied by another craftsman who used another human skull to guide him in making some features more realistic. But this craftsman must have had some knowledge of anatomy, for otherwise the substitution of a false model for the real one would have been very likely to lead to some anatomical abnormalities in his product, although none are actually observed."

Morant also maintained that the British skull is more orthognathous (not having the lower parts of the jaw project) than the average European cranium. For example, an American

Indian skull would probably have a more projecting jawbone and a broader and higher facial skeleton. But interracial variation is so great that such conclusions are highly speculative.

Adrian Digby of the British Museum considered Morant's theories that the two skulls are related and were perhaps of the same origin, and pointed out three possibilities: (1) Morant is correct in assuming that they were made at the same time; (2) the Mitchell-Hedges Skull was made from the original and the British Museum skull was made at a later time from a civilization not acquainted with anatomical details; (3) the British skull was the original and the Mitchell-Hedges skull the copy.

Digby noted that each possibility has complications. If both skulls originated from the same models, why is there so much difference between the two? It is unlikely that the same civilization had such a drastic change of facial characteristics in the course of its history.

He also pointed out that the stylistic differences were not contemporary. "This means that the original 'source' skull was a particularly important skull, probably belonging to a culture hero or warrior, a 'museum piece,' as it were, to which various craftsmen would have access; or alternatively, that the skull was the property of a particular family of craftsmen, and that one model was made by a descendant of the maker of the others."

Both Dr. Morant and the later forensic

reconstruction identify the skulls as feminine, so it is impossible to assume they were representations of a male hero.

In their examination carried out in the 1930s, it was found that in neither case were there any traces of identifiable tool marks, and it is certain that neither specimen was made with steel tools.

The idea that the British Museum skull is a copy of the Mitchell-Hedges Skull raises more puzzling questions. The British skull is "traditionally correct" in that it is most like other skulls, particularly Mexican and South American representations. Digby felt that the Mitchell-Hedges Skull was "improved on . . . But it is extraordinary that anybody wishing to carve a skull out of rock crystal, and taking a real skull as his model, should modify its dimensions to fit those of another crystal skull which he would see was but a poor copy of nature. It shows a perverted ingenuity such as one would expect to find in a forger, but the Mitchell-Hedges Skull bears no traces of recent [Metal Age] workmanship; so this suggestion may almost certainly be dismissed."

The article in the *Man* journal concludes with the comments of H.J. Braunholts of the British Museum: "The cranium [of the British Museum skull] has a perfectly smooth contour, the eyes are circular, and the teeth merely indicated. These peculiarities are in accordance with the general character of ancient Mexican

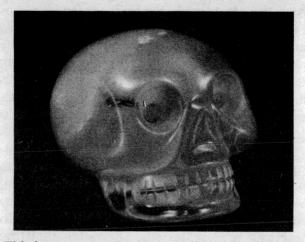

This is a more modern, less realistic crystal skull. It is much smaller than human sized, measuring only 2 1/2 inches high, 2 1/2 wide inches wide, and 3 3/8 inches long. Found in Mexico, it is now at the Seattle Art Museum.

art. It would be hard to quote a single specimen [in] which anatomical detail is fully and faithfully recorded without some degree of 'stylization.' This is particularly the case with the Aztec stone masks and figures of deities, most of which are highly conventional."

The Mitchell-Hedges Skull pays "considerable attention to the correct rendering of detail; minor protuberances on the cranium are carefully modeled . . . such realism seems beyond the ordinary range of Aztec art, and gives the skull the character almost of an anatomical study in a scientific age."

Digby later changed his views and believes that both skulls were made for the same purpose at approximately the same time. He thinks they are most likely pre-Columbian and might belong to some Masonic cult. He does not think there is any likelihood that they were ever of Japanese origin, as some have suggested.

Age of M-H Crystal Skull?

Dorland believes he has found evidences of two distinct stages of evolution in the Crystal Skull's physical construction. First, there was the rough cut—the stage in which the British Museum skull is at. The second stage was the detailing of the Skull's features and the intricate carving of a series of lenses and prisms into the base of the Skull, across the center of the brain cavity, and at the rear of the eye sockets. Even though experts at the British Museum and other institutions had been inspecting the Mitchell-Hedges Skull for years, these surprising details were never noticed until Dorland came into possession of it.

The Mitchell-Hedges Skull has been tentatively identified as Mayan because it was found in Mayan territory. However, Dorland estimates that the Skull could be centuries older than that. If so, it must belong to a civilization that existed long before the Mayans flourished in Mesoamerica.

Unfortunately, there is no conclusive way to determine "when" the skulls were made. Rock crystal cannot be subjected to carbon-14 dating tests. This method only works for organic materials such as bone or wood fossils.

Also, quartz crystal does not change with age like other materials. Carbon-14 dating is inaccurate when it comes to dating prehistorical objects. It can be in error as much as 50 per cent for objects that are five thousand years and older. In addition, quartz crystal does not corrode, become brittle, attract organisms, or acquire a patina. Centuries pass without affecting it.

There is a slight possibility that the location of the original quarry could be determined using some special dating and analytical techniques. This would be impractical and extremely expensive, however. Even this would not provide any conclusive answers, because this information would help to date the crystal only, not when the Crystal Skull was made.

Aztec Skull in Paris Museum

There is yet a third authenticated crystal skull that can be viewed in Paris at the Musee de L'Homme, Palais de Chaillot.

It is believed to represent Mictlantecutli, the Aztec god of death.

This skull measures approximately 4 5/16 inches in height. The lower part of it measures 5 7/8 inches, and it weighs 5 pounds, 8 1/2 ounces.

As you can see from the photo, it is undesirable to look at, and most who see it have an instant aversion to it.

Aztec Skull. The caption of this exhibit reads: "Aztec civilization. Probably 15th century. Death's head in polished quartz probably representing the god of death." This gruesome-looking Aztec skull can be found at the Musee de L'Homme in Paris.

At the side of the skull is a groove and a retaining ring, or chunk. This was for the purpose of fitting a staff with a forked end into the grooves of the skull. The overseer priest would have this impressive skull-topped staff in his possession on the Aztec celebration(?) day of "Skinning Alive."

The god honored was Xipe Totec, the Lord of the Flayed One. (Xipe symbolized spring, flowers, and especially maize, which the Aztecs used as food and for making alcoholic beverages.)

Xipe wore an unusual costume on this day—the skin of a freshly flayed captive. His priest would skin the chosen captive alive, and then don the human skin by fitting the skin over his own, leaving the hands and feet complete and flopping. Then he would dance and celebrate the successful springtime. This grisly ritual was done to materialize a fruitful crop and to insure its harvest.

Neither of the other two crystal skulls found in the Paris or London museums can begin to compare in beauty and magnitude to the Mitchell-Hedges Crystal Skull. They are certainly useful to look at, for their comparison vividly reveals the contrasts in the three, and shows the viewer how much more pleasing it is to view the Mitchell-Hedges Skull and to reflect on its mystery and magic.

It would seem that if the M-H Skull was constructed for a beneficial purpose, it would be worthwhile to pursue the study of it.

**Xipe Totec, the Lord of the Flayed One. This draw-
ing shows a priest being dressed with a human skin
to represent Xipe.**

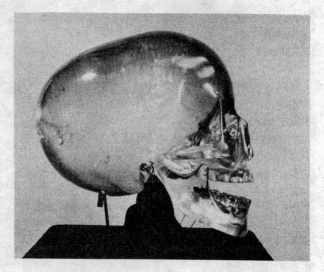

Scientific model of Skull showing how the M-H Skull can be supported on a stand. Long ago a hole was drilled in the bottom of its base, and two holes were drilled on either side of the jaw, allowing ancient priests to manipulate the Skull into a "talking oracle" using rods or wires to move the jaw up and down.

Chapter Seven

ATLANTIS

When F.A. Mitchell-Hedges and his adopted daughter Anna found the Crystal Skull in Lubaantun, he was actually on a search for remnants of the lost legendary civilization of Atlantis.

In 1935, *The New York American* printed a headline saying: "Atlantis Was No Myth, But the Cradle of Civilization, Declares Hedges."

Mitchell-Hedges said, "Atlantis existed. Its engulfment caused 'The Flood,' a cataclysm that wiped out millions. Included was this advanced cultural race. Here upon Atlantis was the 'Cradle of Civilization,' which we follow to this day, land of origin of the races of America."

Even as a young boy the excitement of adventure and the lure of finding lost civilizations was almost an obsession to F.A. Mitchell-Hedges. He grew into a tall, spare man who invariably was seen with a pipe clenched between thin, tight lips. He was a firm believer in independence at any cost, and was always restless, wanting to be in the thick of adventure. Until the day he died, he believed he had found Atlantis and had pieced together mankind's early past.

The Destruction of Atlantis

Otto Heinrich Muck was born in Vienna, and served in WW I. Engineer, inventor, author, he published articles on biological, geological and cancer problems. He patented 2000 inventions that were used by leading industrialists. In WW II he was the inventor of the U-boat snorkel and a member of the Peenemunde Rocket Research Team. After the war he was credited with many inventions in the nutritional field. He died in 1956. His book *The Secret of Atlantis* was published in Germany in 1976, and consequently was translated and published in 1978 by Times Books.

In this deeply researched, scholarly book, Muck builds fact upon fact in a logical, scientific manner which shows how Atlantis once existed geologically, how it was destroyed and when, and how the terrible aftermath had worldwide effects. In conclusion, he draws on historical myths to verify his deductions regarding the catastrophe.

The following excerpt was taken from *The Secret of Atlantis* :

"At 8 P.M., on June 5th, 8498 B.C., the core

parts of Asteriod "A" punched the first decisive hole in the fracture zone of the Atlantic Ridge. The forces of hell were let loose. Through two newly formed vents the glowing red-hot magma shot up at terrific speed and mixed with the liquid above it—the waters of the Atlantic. This created all the conditions for a submarine volcanic eruption of the greatest violence. The fracture seam was torn apart. The bottom of the sea burst open. All existing volcanoes were activated and new vents formed. Terrestrial fire and ocean water became embroiled in ever-increasing volume. Magma mixed with the steam. The chain of fire ran all the way between the two continents from the Beerenberg Volcano on Jan Mayan in the north to Tristan De Cunha in the south."

Beginning with Plato's accounts of Atlantis, Muck comments on the accuracy of the physical description of the Western Atlantic, though its existence completely contradicted the popular belief held about the Earth in Plato's time.

With the discovery and conquest of the New World, attention again turned to Atlantis. Francis Bacon specified Brazil as the continent mentioned; others agreed with him. In 1665, Fr. Athanasius Kircher, a Jesuit, discerned summits of submerged Atlantic ridges in the Azores and drew a map of Atlantis—resembling a pear with its stem pointing southwest.

The Gulf Stream and Atlantis

The Gulf Stream is seven times longer than the Amazon and larger than all the rivers of the world combined. It originates as a westward current of warm tropical water between West Africa and South America, and enters the Caribbean and the Gulf of Mexico with the Easterly trades. It is then deflected and leaves the east coast of North America as a warm westerly current which flows past the Azores and the British Isles as far as northern Norway. The warm waters of the Gulf Stream combine with the humidity of the warm winds that drive it along and bring mild, wet weather to western Europe as far as the extreme north of the continent. (Labrador, unaffected by the Gulf Stream, is subarctic though at the same latitude as England.)

In northeastern America a crop like rye, nonresistant to frost, can only be cultivated up to 50 degrees north. In Norway, it can be cultivated up to a 20 degree higher latitude. This is also true of wheat and potato crops, and the northern limits beyond which horses, mules, and sheep cannot be kept. The inhospitable arctic regions begin at 55 degrees latitude in eastern America, but in Norway they do not start until 70 degrees north.

The general direction of the isotherms (same mean annual temperature) of the North Atlantic region follow the Gulf Stream. The 32 F degree isotherm leaves the east coast of America at about a latitude of 50 degrees north, but it does not turn southward until it reaches the

Arctic Circle at about 75 degrees north. This bulge far into the north above northwestern Europe clearly shows the privileged, one-sided position given this area by the Gulf Stream.

What would happen if the Gulf Stream failed? It would mean that the climate of northwestern Europe would undergo a radical change, and would become normal for that latitude. The isotherms would run from west to east, more or less parallel to the lines of latitude as they do now in North America and Asia. This is offered as a hypothesis, but if the climate conditions postulated by such a change could be shown to have occurred, that would be evidence that the Gulf Stream was not flowing along northwestern Europe.

During the Pleistocene Epoch of the Earth's history, there was about the same cover of ice to the east and the west of the Atlantic. Both continents were buried under huge ice caps that occasionally reached as far as 50 degrees north latitude. The limits of glaciation leave their mark in the form of piled up rock called terminal moraines. The belts of terminal moraines found in Canada and Europe, which indicate the southern limit of advance of inland ice sheets, clearly show that during the Ice Age northwestern Europe did not enjoy a better climate than northeastern America. Thus we conclude that the Gulf Stream did not reach northwest Europe during that time.

The Gulf Stream, a current mightier than

that of all the rivers on Earth combined, flowed during an entire geological era into the Atlantic but did not flow out of it. It does not lose itself in the ocean, therefore it must have encountered a barrier that later disappeared. Not long after it veers away from the east coast of North America, the Gulf Stream attains a width of between 350-500 miles. To block it effectively a barrier must have been 500-620 miles long, measured at right angles to the current. The floor of the Atlantic is not level, but exhibits a marked relief. There is a long, massive submarine reef that extends from Iceland in the north to the Atlantic shelf in the south. In one place this ridge widens out into what has the appearance of a great submarine mountain, out of which sharp peaks rise to form the Azores. The mountain Pico Alto rises to 7600 feet above sea level, 20,000 feet above the ocean floor. This submarine massif, if formerly an island, could have blocked the Gulf Stream.

Geologists and paleontologists differ as to exactly when the Earth moved into the fifth geological age. Experts using different criteria place the time from 20,000 years ago to 8,000. De Geer, counting the bands in the Swedish varved clay, arrived at an "optimum" of 12,000 years, or 10,000 B.C., the time when Atlantis was supposed to have sunk beneath the sea. Thus Muck concludes that the Azores are the remnants of Atlantis.

He cites further evidence in the migratory patterns of eels. Originating in the Sargasso Sea, where they are protected by the seaweed, American eels spawn in the western part and the European eels in the eastern part. The European eels swim, not to the nearest land, but drift with the Gulf Stream across the Atlantic to distant Europe. This long and dangerous journey takes three years. Only the female eels enter the fresh water, which they need to become sexually mature. The male eels do not enter the fresh water but remain in the sea. After two years the sexes reunite, return to the Sargasso Sea in the very short time of 140 days, mate, and the cycle begins again.

Muck postulates that this dangerous journey is an example of the survival instinct that, when thwarted, became a danger to the species. When the fresh water streams of Atlantis were available to the eels, they were protected by the seaweed beds. When Atlantis was destroyed, they were still driven by instinct to make the long and dangerous journey to the fresh water.

Muck believed Cro-Magnon man came to Europe in hunting parties from the west and exterminated the Neanderthal. In the New World he sees the Atlanteans as proto-American Indian. He quotes Herbert Wendt's *Ich suchte Adam (I Looked for Adam)*:

"Since Chester Stock speculated on the footprints found at Carson City, Nevada, numerous human skeletons and relics of civilization have been discovered throughout the American continent from Minnesota to the Strait of Magellan. These proto-Americans belonged without exception to the species Homo sapiens; they combine the characteristics of Cro-Magnon Man with Mongoloid and Red Indian traits, and can be dated fairly accurately with the aid of radio carbon and the fluorine test. None of the skeletons had been in the American ground longer than 12,000 years."

Muck maintains that Wegeners' continental drift theory of a match between continents is only accurate if the "hole" left northeast of Mexico is filled in with the now-submerged Atlantic Ridge.

In the northern Atlantic where it borders on the North Polar Sea, a Norwegian Polar expedition working from shell and otoliths of animals inhabiting shallow waters (now found at depths of 3300 to 8200 feet) concluded that the area had dropped 6560 feet very suddenly in the most recent geological period, otherwise the shallow sea animals would have had time to escape to the continental shelf.

Iceland was then about four times the size it is today. An area of ocean the size of a continent, several million square miles, sunk 3300 to 6560 feet. A tachylite (black glassy basalt) recovered from the ocean floor on Telegraph Plateau was formed by a land volcano. Mineralogical classification shows it was less than 15,000 years old, or from 13,000 B.C. The American geophysicist Piggot recovered core samples of nine feet ten inches in the Atlantic that included two zones of very rich volcanic ash. The two topmost of the volcanic strata are found above the topmost glacial stratum, which indicates that this volcanic catastrophe occurred in postglacial times. Similar cores collected near Newfoundland also contained ash.

But a core sample taken near the Atlantic Ridge where Muck has placed Atlantis differed considerably from those taken on either side of the central ridge. It was unusually short, with a sediment no deeper than 3 1/8 inches. Professor Peterson in *Atlantis and Atlantic* says, "The pipe seems to have struck hard material, probably rock, of which no samples were obtained. . . It can therefore not be entirely ruled out that the Mid-Atlantic Ridge, where the sample originated, was above sea level up to about 10,000 years ago and did not subside to its present depth until later."

Asteroid Craters

The ocean floor in the Atlantic east of North America's southeast coast shows an abnormality: two great holes, 23,000 feet deep. Muck regards these deep sea holes as the unhealed scars left by two deep wounds inflicted on the Earth's crust by the impact of a celestial body of considerable size: an asteroid.

In the 1930s an aerial survey first called attention to the Carolina crater field. The area around Charleston is dotted with bays, holes created by the impact of a meteorite that fell about 10,000 years ago. The famous Tungaska meteor that fell in Siberia in 1908 is estimated to have weighed one million tons or more. The enormous amounts of meteoric dust that were introduced into the sky produced clouds all over Western Siberia and Europe that turned the light of day into a dim reddish twilight. Muck estimates the force of the meteorite that destroyed Atlantis was 200,000,000 times greater.

He calls on several myths that perhaps give poetic descriptions of the cataclysm. One, from the Chilam Balam, written in Maya language in Roman script, states: "A fiery rain fell, ashes fell, rocks and trees crashed to the ground. He smashed trees and rocks asunder . . . and the Great Snake was torn from the sky and skin and pieces of its bones fell onto earth. Arrows struck orphans and old men, widowers and widows, who were alive, yet did not have the strength to live. And they were buried on the sandy seashore, then the waters rose in a terrible flood. And with the Great Snake the sky fell in and the dry land sank into the sea."

This description originates in a country not far from where the Carolina Meteorite struck. The imagery of the Great Snake torn from the sky is very vivid. The asteroid with the luminous trails of gasses flooding from its head must have indeed looked like a snake composed of suns and stars that was brighter than the Sun.

And the terrible apparition did appear to have a mouth that was breathing fire, and it did suddenly explode into fragments. As the account says, "its skin and pieces of its bones fell onto the earth."

The asteroid fell in the worst possible place—one of the thinnest, most sensitive areas of the Earth's crust. It fell on a fracture zone dotted with volcanoes, the Atlantic Ridge. Two holes were punched into the red-hot depths below the Earth's crust, and Muck estimates this set off a cosmic explosive charge equal to 30,000 hydrogen bombs.

When the red-hot magma shot up and mixed with the waters of the Atlantic, it created a submarine volcanic eruption of the greatest possible violence. The volcanic eruptions ran along the entire fracture chain in a huge chain reaction. As long as the fracture seam continued to burst open, magma, water vapor, and gases continued to increase. The magma blown high into the atmosphere did not fall back. It was widely dispersed by the storms that were a by-product.

A magma depression was created below the center of the Atlantic basin. Comparing it statistically to the Krakatoa explosion, Muck estimates that the magma level dropped about two to two and one-half miles in 24 hours. The thunder of eruptions and explosions gradually died away and the red-hot surface closed and the ocean flooded in. Thus: "In a single dreadful day and a single dreadful night" Atlantis disappeared.

The resulting cloud of dust, gases, and volcanic ash played havoc all over the Earth. Animals and vegetation died, some instantly frozen, others from asphyxiation. The torrential rains flooded all of the Earth. The darkness would not be fully expelled for two thousand years.

Muck postulates that, as the Romans began counting their calendar from the founding of Rome and the Christians from the birth of Christ, the Mayan calendar began with the destruction of Atlantis—a day of horror, a day that shook the world, a day that introduced a new climatic era, June 5, 8498 B.C.

Atlantis and Crystals

When the fitted stones forming a roadway were found in the shallow water near Bimini in 1969, it came as no surprise to the followers of Edgar Cayce, "The Sleeping Prophet," who had predicted it would happen in that very year. Cayce, a Bible-reading fundamentalist, gave trance readings, all carefully recorded, from the 1920s to the 1940s. Cayce conducted numerous "life readings" which ranged back over the millenia to the oceanic civilization of Atlantis. Remarkably, many of his "readings" contain information that Cayce (or anyone else) could not have understood at the time he gave them. In his waking state Cayce was often troubled and puzzled by the material he produced while in trance, but he has proved to be one of the most accurate and remarkable seers of our time.

Francis Joseph, using intuition and careful, in-depth research, has carefully pieced together a historic trail leading from Atlantis to the Crystal Skull. (For more information on Atlantis see *The Destruction of Atlantis* by Francis Joseph from Atlantis Research Publishers, Olympia, IL) In the article "The Crystals of Atlantis" he states:

"Of all the mysteries of that most mysterious place, none are more puzzling than the crystals of Atlantis. Were they mystic symbols of religious and political power? Or were they mineral storage batteries for arcane mechanical and psychic powers? Do they still lie under unknown fathoms of ocean with the broken ruins of Atlantis? Or has at least one of their number (exquisitely carved in the shape of a human skull) been found in a Central American dig?

"The opulent island-capital of the maritime empire that once stretched from the Aegean Sea to the Mid-Atlantic, Atlantis was abruptly annihilated by a natural catastrophe equivalent to a nuclear event that sank her beneath the waves and into legend. Part of that legend begins with psychic information that Edgar Cayce provided:

'What is now the Sahara was (during the Atlanteans' migration from their sunken homeland in the West to the Nile Valley in the East) an inhabited land and very fertile' (364-13,1939).

"Only since the 1950s were geologists able to confirm that well into the 2nd Millennium B.C., the Sahara was indeed fertile, although

Edgar Cayce, one of America's best known and most accurate psychics. He delivered many prophecies and gave helpful life readings for thousands of individuals.

caught in a losing battle with the encroaching desert. A people now known to the archaeologists as the Pastoralists, with many cultural elements in common with the Archaic Dynasty Egyptians of the Lower Nile, prospered in what is today unlivable wasteland.

"Cayce characterized Atlantis as the Motherland of Civilization, where the earliest religion was a solar-oriented monotheism (Sons of the Law of One); the symbolic, sacred numerals five and six pervaded its culture; and several geological upheavals destroyed the island over a period of time.

"Cayce reported that the 'initiates' of Atlantis (Reading # 440-5; 1933) engineered and manipulated precious power crystals for the production of galvanic and spiritual energies. The crystals were so potent they were in large part responsible for the Atlanteans' advanced technology. Later, in Atlantis history when crystals were improperly used, they contributed to the final destruction of the island-empire. The crystals were housed in an oval temple, the roof of which rolled back to admit light from the sun and stars which activated the 'white fire stones.' (Reading # 440-5; 1933)

"The descriptions of the crystals' functions may be understood literally or symbolically. Atlas, the chief mythic figure of Atlantis, was portrayed in Greek myth (Appolodorus, Hesiod, etc.) as the founder of astrology. The relationship between the Atlanteans' sacred crystals and the stars to which they attached such importance may have held important cultic significance. The possession of the crystals by the 'initiates' or the high priests would be, symbolically, possession of the stars themselves. The resulting politico-religious power inherent in the crystals may then be appreciated, and perhaps this was the real power that Cayce intended to describe.

"Igneous rocks forming far below the surface of the earth are usually crystalline. Extrusive, or volcanic rocks, are sometimes entirely glassy, and such pure, glassy crystals are the results of rapidly cooled magma. The island of Atlantis was an enormous volcano, Mt. Atlas. If the Atlanteans possessed the abundance of crystals Cayce indicated, a volcanic environment would have been necessary for their collection. It is doubtful Cayce understood the volcanic origins of crystal, nor was he able to make any connection between their magnetic nature and the geologic character of Mt. Atlas. He does associate the final destruction of Atlantis with the crystals, tying the cataclysm to a volcanic event.

"The typical termination of a quartz crystal is a hexagonal prism, each of the six facets the shape of an isosceles triangle. This crystal embodies the sacred numerals of Atlantis, five and six, and terminates in a pyramid. A bipyramid appears when, sitting on the reflecting surface of a mirror or water, a pyramid perfectly reflects its inverted image. According to some researchers (Robert West, *Serpent in the Sky*; Peter

Lemesurier, *The Great Pyramid Decoded*; Francis Joseph, *The Survivors of Atlantis*), if the Great Pyramid of Giza is, as part of its function, a memorial to the holy, ancestral, sunken mountain of Atlas, the inherent symbolism of crystal becomes apparent.

"The crystal theme of Atlantis echoes in the surviving traditions of peoples touched by the influence of the once powerful oceanic civilization. In the Welsh poem the "Spoils of Annwn," King Arthur and his men escape from a rapidly sinking island in the Mid-Atlantic. The capital of the island was the magnificent Caer Wydyr, 'The Glass Fortress.' Nannius, the 12th century chronicler, wrote in his *Historium Brittanum* of the splendid city, head of an ancient, seaborn empire, swallowed up by the Atlantic for the pagan practices of its unrepentant inhabitants. He called the city Turris Vitrea, 'the Tower of Glass,' bringing to mind Cayce's description of the special tower with its roll-back dome in which the sacred crystals were kept. (Incidentally, Cayce's 'life readings' regularly refer to the crystals as 'cut glass', 'white stones', 'faceted glass', etc.)

"The Druid priests told Julius Caesar that the Gauls believed their ancestors came to Europe unremembered millennia before from the 'Isle of Glass Towers,' long drowned in the Atlantic far-off Iberian shores. The survivors' legendary landfall was Oporto, which the Romans consequently referred to as the Port of the Gauls, or Portus Galle, from which came modern-day Portugal.

"The early 2nd century A.D. Lucian of Samosata, in his *Historia Vara*, described a large, highly civilized island-city that sank into the Atlantic 'ages before our own.' Before it disappeared forever beneath the waves, one of its outstanding features was a 'crystal building.'

"The Old Irish *Voyage of Maildune* contains a description of Atlantis which, detail for detail, is very close to Plato's account, but it contains this additional piece of information: the inner wall of the great island palace Maildune visited was profusely decorated with crystal. This inner wall, according to Plato, surrounded the Temple of Poseidon, the Atlantean Holy-of-Holies, again recalling Cayce's 'life readings.'

"Plato does not mention crystal in his Atlantis narrative, the *Timaeus* and the *Critias*. Then again, perhaps he does it under a different name: 'orichalcum.' The item's precise identity had long been a controversial stumbling block for scholars. Plato said it was 'that which is now only a name,' and was used by the Atlanteans to decorate their temples, palaces, walls, and monumental public works.

"The word 'crystal' derives from the Greek *crystallos*, or 'clear ice,' but this does not necessarily mean Plato was personally familiar with it, because much of Athens' import trade from the Western Mediterranean (crystal came from the Lipari Islands, just northeast of Sicily) was constantly menaced by Etruscan and Carthaginian pirates. Hence, crystal might have seemed to him 'that which is now only a name, and was then something more than a name,' his orichalcum.

"On the other side of the Atlantic Ocean, where oral traditions of 'White Chiefs' arriving on American shores from a great, drowned island are abundant among the Plains Indians, the Pima flood-story recalls how South Doctor 'held magic crystals in his left hand,' as he guided the shaken survivors to safety in a new land.

"Cayce said (Reading #440-5; 1933): 'About the firestone—the entity's activities then made such applications as dealt both with the constructive as well as the destructive forces of that period.'

"The Olmecs, who first brought civilization to Mesoamerica about 1500 B.C. and whose Atlantean origins have been capably demonstrated (*Atlantis in America*, Lewis Spence) used polished stones as mirrors to light fires. Texcatlipoca's (smoking mirror) animal disguise was the jaguar, its spotted skin represented the starry sky. In his mirror Texcatlipoca saw everything—past, present and future, including the deeds and thoughts of men. The Atlantean features of this god are clear, from his sovereignty over a world cataclysm to his identification with the heavenly bodies, signifying his astrological character, an aspect emphasized by his mirror. Tezcatlipoca's Old World correspondent may be seen at Turin's Egyptian Museum, which houses a statue of Anen, an astrologer, wearing a cheetah skin, the spots of which have been reworked into five-pointed stars. The skin is fastened by the gold mask of the cheetah's face. Lindsay reproduces a drawing of a Dionysiac officient wrapped in a lion skin spotted with stars, as she appeals for an omen for Dionysus. These vital cultural comparisons not only underscore very ancient pre-Columbian contacts between Mesoamerica and European civilizations, but they thematically imply the Atlantean identity of those contacts.

"Texcatlipoca found his mortal counterpart in Peru. An early king of the Incas, Pachacu'tec, 'Transformer of the Globe,' was said to have envisioned his future greatness in a sacred crystal bequeathed to his family by Kon-Tiki-Viracocha, the tall, red-bearded, blue-eyed, white founding father of Andean civilization from a distant, sunken homeland. If nothing else, the crystal motif, its mythic association with prophecy and distinctly Atlantean elements in pre-Columbian America, represents a cultural continuity suggestive of a thematic link with the Old World civilizations of Europe through Atlantis.

"But the most outstanding appearance of the Atlantean crystal motif in America took place in British Honduras, Belize, where Cayce said important artifacts of Atlantis origin were to be recovered. Mitchell-Hedges believed in

Atlantis and was searching for it when he discovered Lubaantun.

"Ymir, the giant of Norse legend, had his skull transformed into the vault of heaven with its stars of destiny, and we recall Pachacu'tec, the Inca monarch, glimpsing his own future in an ancestral crystal. Atlas, the first king of Atlantis, was the founder of astrology, and the Mayas were no less avid astrologers than their Atlantean ancestors.

"Is the Crystal Skull the 'terrible, mighty crystal' from the lost island civilization of Atlantis? Was it carried from the doomed, sinking city by its high priests to the dry sanctuary of Mesoamerica, as Edgar Cayce described?"

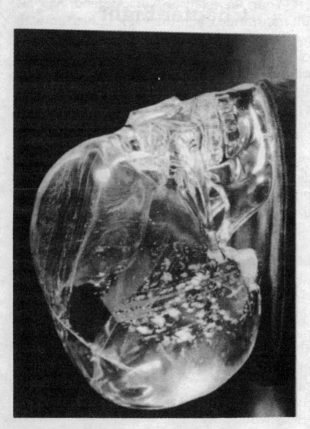

Full side view of M-H Crystal Skull showing naturally occurring inclusions in it.

Chapter Eight

MESOAMERICA

If one accepts the myth of Atlantis, then the crystal skulls are easily explained. They are some of the programmed crystals planted when the followers of the Law of One knew that Atlantis was breaking up. That explanation, too, would account for the strong similarities among the ancient known civilizations—the pyramids, the exact tables of the movements of the planet Venus (this is found in the earliest Sumerian writings as well as in one of the few translated Mayan glyphs).

Interpretations from the *Popul Voh* (a book written in Quiche Maya using Spanish script) indicates that in Central America, the Maya myth gave Palenque as the place where man originated. Interestingly enough Palenque is the geographic center of the land mass of South America.

Peru, too, when viewed from the point of the Atlantean myth offers some interesting facts.

There massive stones weighing many tons were mortised together into buildings that stand today with impenetrable joints. Under an absolute monarch, the Inca ran the country very efficiently. The people were well cared for and fed under government supervision of crops. When a crop failure occurred, they were supplied from government-controlled storehouses or relocated en masse to new locations. The village would be kept intact with no disruption of leadership or mores. The incredible engineering of the roads—on straight lines using viaducts and bridges—is inexplicable in an unscientific society. A man running cross-country will detour a long way up and down a stream to find an easy crossing.

The ruling class of the Inca never intermarried with the main populace. This hints at a technologically advanced people conquering a more backward people and holding the divisions of culture in a very benevolent way. This would be an unusual course of events. Most usually the intermingling of bloodlines occurs quickly even if class distinctions are held with a conquering people. (Witness the emergence of the mestizo in Mexico.) The ruling Inca believed themselves to each be a god, descended from gods.

In looking at the rich and diverse cultures that make up present-day Mexico, it is well to remember that their entire history has been interpreted through European eyes and European cultural biases.

Beginning in the first decade after the

arrival of the Spaniards, Fray Bernardino de Sahagun' employed a battery of scribes to record all that elderly Indian informants could tell of what they remembered or had been told about their civilization. There are thousands of folios in the Nahuatl language written by natives after the conquest extant today in European museums.

Drawing extensively on these documents, Miguel Leon-Portilla has compounded an in-depth study of Nahuatl philosophy which he believes stemmed from the ancient doctrines and traditions of the Teotihuacans and the Toltecs. In *Aztec Thought and Culture*, he tells us: "In the manner of other peoples, the earth was conceived by the Mexicans as a large wheel or disc completely surrounded by water. This plat-form encompassed by water was called ring or complete circle. Erroneously early historians designated the central part of Mexico as the plateau of Ana'huac. To the ancients this term carried the meaning of land situated 'at the edge of the water' (between oceans). They called this water divine water, for it merged with the heav-ens at the horizon. The Nahuatl believed they had come from the sea, from the region of light (East) and their journey had ended at the Atlantic coast."

From Mesoamerica, Frank Waters in his book *Mexico Mystique* states: "The creation myth of the Quiche Maya attests to the belief that mankind was first possessed of perfect and complete cosmic knowledge. It relates that the Creator and Maker, **Tepeu** and Gucumatz, the Forefathers, and the **Heart** of Heaven, usually known as the Huracan, in council tried three times to create human beings on earth. All were destroyed, only the fourth attempt being successful."

Legend of Quetzalcoatl

Among the many diverse cultures of Mesoamerica, one belief dominates: that of the god, Quetzalcoatl. The name is derived from *quetzal*, a rare, brilliantly green bird found only in the highlands of Chiapas and Guatemala, and *coatl*, or serpent. Thus, literally, plumed serpent. The earliest myth of Quetzalcoatl that has been translated is of a god, wise, pure and good. He appeared among the people to teach them the arts and sciences and to give them a calendar. He fell into temptation, drank, and sank into carnality. In repentance he cast himself into the ritual flames. The names of Quetzalcoatl are legion: Kulkulcan, Gucumatz, Plumed Serpent, Ehcatl the god of the wind. As Lord of the Dawn, the morning star, he was the personification of the planet Venus.

To the Mesoamericans, a quetzal feather is something precious. Coatl also means twin, thus: precious twin, a possible reference to Venus, as both the evening and morning star. In the myth, Quetzalcoatl, with his twin, or double, Xolotl, visited the Land of the Dead. On the eighth day he ascended as Lord of the Dawn, the morning star. As Venus, he repeats this ritual journey, appearing as the evening star and reappearing as the morning star.

One of the few glyph records that have been translated from the Maya is a table of the movements of the planet Venus. As the morning star is represented by Quetzalcoatl, the evening star is called Xolotl, his twin brother. Xolotl is often represented as a fleshless skull. In Aztec and Nahuatl legend he is called a sorcerer. As Quetzalcoatl represents the daylight journey of Venus, he represents the night journey through the underworld. As Quetzalcoatl, the enduring spiritual principle is resurrected, so also is included his earthly double, or twin, Xolotl.

Xolotl also symbolizes fire and water—the fire that falls from the sky, or lightning. Xolotl is shown in the codice *Borgia*, now in the library of the Vatican, as born of water, as is lightning from a cloud. (The Codices are esoteric paintings on animal skins.)

The *Seldon Codex* depicts a mask of a fleshless skull, Venus as Xolotl, journeying to the Land of the Dead. C. A. Burland in *Montezuma, Lord of the Aztecs* attributes the British Museum crystal skull as a representation of Mictlantecuhtli, Lord of the Land of the Dead. But Alfonso Caso states: "The myth relates that Quetzalcoatl and his twin brother, Xolotl, descended to the world of the

Quetzalcoatl

A god of the Toltecs and Aztecs. Quetzalcoatl is represented as a plumed or feathered serpent god.

dead. When they arrived they made their plea before Mictlantecuhtli, the god of the dead." It seems more likely that the Crystal Skull would have been made in the likeness of Xolotl, twin brother of Quetzalcoatl, creator of man, rather than in the likeness of Mictlantecuhtli.

Alfonso Caso, one of the greatest contemporary historians, states: "As the god of life, Quetzalcoatl appears as the constant benefactor of mankind, and after having created man, he sought to nourish him. He discovered corn, which he gave to man. He taught man how to polish jade and other precious stones, and how to locate deposits of them. He showed him how to weave multicolored fabrics from the miraculous cotton that grew in different colors; he taught him how to do mosaic work with feathers of the quetzal bird, the bluebird, the hummingbird, the macaw and others. But above all, he taught man science, thereby endowing him with the means to measure time and study the movements of the stars; he taught him how to arrange a calendar and devised ceremonies and fixed certain days for prayers and sacrifices."

As the Biblical prophecies foretold of a Prophet from the line of David, so the Mayan calendar forecast the birth of a child: Ce Acatl Topiltzen Quetzalcoatl. He was born on the day One Reed in the Year One Reed, by their Ceremonial Calendar. The general course of his life was laid out in the prophecies, but that life was only one portion of a vast epic. He has been called the greatest figure in the ancient history of Mesoamerica, with a code of ethics and a love for the arts and sciences.

Laurette Sejourne states in *Burning Water*: "His essential role as founder of Nahuatl culture was never questioned by any of the historians of the 16th and 17th centuries, who always state that just as our era began with Christ, so that of the Aztecs and their predecessors began—approximately at the same time—with Quetzalcoatl. His image, the plumed serpent, had for pre-Columbian peoples the same evocative force as the crucifix did for Christianity."

There are two interpretations of Quetzalcoatl: one is the man, and one is the legend or deity. The historical man has been attributed with all of the characteristics of the mythical god, Quetzalcoatl. (Historians place the dates of his life from 747 A.D. to 799 A.D., but according to Jose Arguelles in *Surfers of the Zuvuya*, he lived from 947 A.D. to 999 A.D.)

The legends of the god Quetzalcoatl and the man Quetzalcoatl are intermixed and open to various interpretations by historians. The Aztecs, a very primitive and warlike tribe ruled by sorcerers, invaded the Valley of Mexico. Instead of destroying, they assimilated the ancient cultures and in time came to call the older civilizations their ancestors. But, having taken possession of a cultural heritage, the Aztec still venerated "Those who were first inhabitants of this land."

Sejourne states: "In tracing Aztec origins, the chroniclers speak of the ancient Nahuas and attribute to them the foundation, at about the beginning of the Christian era, of the religious system that nourished pre-Columbian Mexico for 1500 years. Archaeological excavations have fully confirmed the accuracy of these texts, having unearthed in the ruins of the first Nahuatl capital evidence of the same gods, the same rituals, the same symbolic language as in the last."

In *Aztec Thought and Culture* Miguel Leon-Portilla comments: "These ancient people were called Toltecs, which in Nahautl means 'master craftsman'." De Sahagun states: "Whatever they turned their hands to was delicate and elegant, all was very good, remarkable and gracious, such as the houses they made beautiful, highly decorated within, of a certain kind of precious stone very green with lime, and those so adorned had a lime highly polished which was a sight to be seen, and stones also, fashioned and stuck together that seemed like a kind of mosaic; with justice were later called exquisite and noteworthy because they possessed such beauty of workmanship and labor. They were inventors of the art of featherwork, and all that was done in ancient times was made with wonderful invention and skill . . .

"The Toltecs had much experience and knowledge in the qualities and virtues of herbs, and they left docketed and named those now used for treating, because they were also physicians and the best in the arts . . . they were the first inventors of medicine . . .

"What they achieved in knowledge of precious stones was so great that, though these were buried in a larger one and below ground, by their natural genius and philosophy they would discover where to find them . . .

"So remarkable were these Toltecs that they knew all mechanical skills and in all of these were unique and exquisite craftsmen, for they were painters, stoneworkers, carpenters, bricklayers, masons, workers in feathers and ceramics, spinners, weavers . . .

"They were so skilled in astronomy . . . that they were the first to take count of and order the days of the year . . .

"They also invented the art of interpreting dreams, and they were so informed and wise that they knew the stars in the heavens, and had given them names and knew their movements and their influence and qualities . . .

"Those Toltecs were good men and drawn to virtue . . . they were tall, larger in body than those who live now . . . They also sang well, and while they sang or danced they used drums and timbrels of wood . . . they played, composed and arranged curious songs out of their heads; they were very devout, and great orators . . .

"The civilization of the Toltec spread all over Mesoamerica and the leader of this great civilization was a king called Quetzalcoatl . . "

To the Nahuatl, the word "face" referred to the ego. The allusion was not anatomical but metaphorical. It described the most individual characteristic of the human being—the very element which removed his anonymity.

Leon-Portilla comments at length on Nahuatl metaphysical and theological ideas. From a poem included in *Toltec-Chichimec History* (circa 1540): "the 'mirror which illumines' is identified with the god of duality, creator of men, whose light illumines all that exists. It should be noted that a clear contrast exists between Tezcatlanextia and Tezcatlipoca (smoking mirror); one illumines, the other obscures with his smoke."

The archaic term for mirror is a crystal or similar device used by diviners, sorcerers, etc. The above myth is the classic story of the battle of light against dark.

It was not until 1932, when Dr. Caso discovered Tomb 7 at Monte Alban (500 B.C.-1469 A.D.) that examples of the artwork described by de Sahagun were found. The Spaniards marveled at the exquisitely detailed and delicate beauty of the goldwork found everywhere in Mesoamerica. It equalled or surpassed any found in the Old World at a time when the arts of the Renaissance flowered. In their greed the

Spaniards melted it all down into ingots for easier transporting.

Given the knowledge of optics, it would seem that the Toltec perhaps had the necessary skill to fashion the skulls. Is it possible that the Mitchell-Hedges Crystal Skull was originally from Atlantis and the other skull a copy made by the Toltecs, not as fine as the original? Unfortunately we will never know for certain.

The surviving art work from Tomb 7, a burial of nine priests, was an exceedingly rich find but it could not have compared to the magnificence of a royal burial. It contained gold and silver jewels, an abundance of jade objects,

Ancient quartz crystal goblet found at Tomb 7 in Monte Alban, Mexico.

turquoise mosaics, necklaces of rock crystal, amber, jet, coral and shells, vessels of silver, alabaster and rock crystal, thousands of pearls, one of which was the size of a pigeon egg, and jaguar bones carved with a perfection to equal the best Chinese and Hindu ivories. One of the most interesting artifacts, from the standpoint of the history of crystal, was a stemmed goblet, carved from rock quartz crystal. Its delicate pedestal base and smooth perfection would grace a contemporary dinner table. Some five inches high, the milky quartz crystal is highly polished and exquisitely smooth.

The Mayan Calendar

Mesoamerica, as no other area of the world, has been dominated by an art motif so stark as the fleshless skull. Their calendar, used by the Olmec, Toltec, Mixtec, and the people of Oaxaca, had a count of 365.2422 days of the year, as compared to the one in use now of 365.2420 days. Aware that the calendar was short of the true year, they kept careful records of the accumulated error.

The Mayan used a "short count" as well— their sacred ritualistic calendar of 260 days. The two calendars meshed and returned to a given starting point every 52 years. Each day of the year had a special significance, and was under the power of a given god. Since a given day and year would not repeat for 52 years, Quetzalcoatl's birth (of the man) on the day One

Reed in the Year One Reed signified that he was born at the beginning of a new cycle.

The 20 days were regarded as gods, and the accompanying numbers held similar rank. The glyph for those day names appears as a stylized portrait of those gods, or as highly conventionalized pictures of attributes or insignia of the deities. The thirteen accompanying numbers equals a combination of 260 days, then the cycle begins again.

Individual combinations of day names and numbers wielded enormous influence over the daily life of the Maya, from prince to peasant. The luck of each day name and number decided when crops should be planted, when wars should be started, whether individuals would be suitably mated, or when marriage should take place. The aspects of the days dominated practically every activity, group, or individual. A rigid system of predestination encompassed the individual because the influence of the day of his birth molded his entire life.

They used a dual numbering system. As we use both Arabic and Roman numerals, they used a bar and dot system and a head variant. The Mayan system was vigesimal (20) rather than decimal (10). The vigesimal system embodied the concept of zero. Known to have been developed in the early Hindu civilizations and diffused throughout the ancient world, the concept of zero did not reach Western Europe until the Arab invasion in the early Middle Ages, several centuries after the Maya had developed their system. The Mayan concept development has been placed somewhere around 200 B.C. The symbol for zero is the glyph of a shell.

In the bar and dot system the bar equals five, the dot one. In the head variant system, a head of a god represented the numbers from one to 13. The number ten was portrayed by a fleshless skull and significantly in relation to the Crystal Skull, this system used the detached skeletal jawbone for the number ten. (The basis for our metric system is, of course, the zero and the digit.) As an example, the head number seven plus the jawbone equaled the sum total of 17. The head number 19 plus the jaw would equal 29.

Mayan Numbering System

The American archaeologist J. T. Goodman, in working to decipher the glyphs, recognized the head of the god of number ten many years ago, and his interpretation of it as the death god has been widely accepted. The principal characteristics are the bared jawbone, the fleshless nose, the % sign on the cheek, the "eye" on the forehead, and the three dots on the upper part of the head.

Of these characteristics only the bared jawbone is constant, but one or more of the remaining ones is usually present. Because of the unusual aspect of the detached lower jawbone of the Crystal Skull, there has been speculation that it was a representation of the death god. However, research does not bear out this interpretation.

The death god—Cimi, Tox, Camel—is the sign for the sixth day. The root name is from the Yucatec word *cimil*, "to die—death." The animal of this day is the cui owl, the Mayan portent of death. According to the *Popul Voh*, the Lords of the Underworld (the Lords of Xilbalba) were 1 Came and 7 Came, and this day name has the same root as the Quiche Maya word for death. This is considered a lucky day.

In Chichen Itza (established around 750 A.D.), on the Yucatan peninsula directly north of Belize, there is still standing an enormous platform with walls some 10 feet high, carved with skull after skull, all different. There is also the Temple of the Warriors, with its huge

Wall of Skulls at Chichen Itza

replica of rattlesnakes and its *chac mool* (statue of a reclining rain god with a bowl on his stomach for containing water, an offering, or the heart of a sacrificial victim), which according to the National Geographic's *The Mysterious Maya*, is circa 1000 A.D.

Both the Maya and the Aztec were obsessed with the 52-year cycle of their religious calendar, now called the "calendar round." The ending of a cycle (the binding up of the bundle of years) was a tremendous event.

In *The Ancient Sun Kingdoms of the Americas* Victor Wolfgang von Hagen states: "Every moment of their lives was involved in the position of the planets. They feared that if the gods were not propitiated they would put an end to the world. Perhaps that was the reason for their obsession with having an almost exact calendar, so that each god at the right moment might have his prayers or the sacrifices meant for him."

At the end of the 52-year period, all cooking utensils were destroyed, no fires were lighted during the five-day dead period (*nemontemi*), no food cooked, and on the last night the people held a vigil to "bundle up the years" and anxiously awaited the word from the priests to see if the sacred fire could be lighted again, and if the world would continue for another 52 years.

Considering these facts, it seems reasonable to conclude that some significant event had caused the beginning of this unusual ceremony of such anguish and fear.

The highly controversial Immanuel Velikovsky developed the theory that Venus was born from Jupiter as a comet in the second millenium. He postulated that this resulted in two catastrophies for Earth, 52 years apart, between 1600 B.C. and 1500 B.C. He maintained that Venus was a comet for seven centuries, described in myth as a serpent with a tail, or a serpent adorned with feathers.

If Velikovsky is correct (many other theories of his have proved true), that would explain the physical basis for the origin of the possibility of extinction at the end of a 52-year cycle. It could also explain the power of the Plumed Serpent Cult, for it was very widespread, reaching as far north as Ohio, as evidenced by the Great Serpent Mound, and the rituals of the Zuni in New Mexico and the Hopi in Arizona.

It is now widely accepted that many voyagers (the Chinese, the Vikings, the Phoenicians) reached the so-called New World long before Cortez found the Aztec Empire. Like Cortez, the Aztecs were the johnny-come-latelys. Having come down into the Valley of Mexico from the north, they conquered the people, but unlike many conquerors, they claimed as their own the rich and wonderful heritage.

They developed a culture of extremes: a ruling class that loved beauty and luxury, advanced education for noblemen, and a philosophy that could state: "A wise man is he who puts a mirror before others; he makes them prudent, cautious, he causes a face (personality) to appear to them." (Leon-Portillo)

On the other extreme, they worshipped some very angry gods who demanded human sacrifice—human hearts' blood to keep the Sun moving.

The inscription above the gateway to the Museum of Anthropology in Mexico City (one of the finest museums of its kind in the world) reads:

Valor and confidence to face the future is found by people in the grandeur of their past. Mexicans look at yourself in the mirror of this splendor. Strangers, know also the unity of human destiny. Civilizations pass, but man has always within him the glory of those who struggled to bring him into being.

Whether the Crystal Skull came from Atlantis and was copied by the Toltecs, or whether its origin is from the stars or from a still undreamed-of source, the message is still the same. Someone left, carved in crystal, a symbol indicating, "Man has always within him the glory of those who struggled to bring him into being."

Chapter Nine

HISTORICAL USES OF QUARTZ CRYSTAL

Crystal was a sacred substance in the mind of ancient man. The word comes from the Greek *krystallos*——clear ice—and it was believed to be frozen holy water that God had spilled from Heaven. It was thought that as it drifted earthward it became frozen into ice in outer space. This holy ice was then miraculously petrified by the guardian angels so that, forevermore, it would remain cold and would not melt and run away. Thus, the holy water was preserved in solid form for the protection and blessing of mankind. There was a universal, almost worldwide belief that the veils in the crystal (the inclusions) were the souls of guardian angels.

Crystal was believed to dispel sorcery, divert the evil eye, and bestow divine power on the wearer. In ancient lands it was the symbol of the water god: Ea in Babylon, Tet in Egypt. We find that water is associated with all the stories of man's beginnings. It is the one thing, after air, that we cannot do without. Perhaps it is because of the association with water that crystal has always been regarded as a sacred substance.

Since time immemorial humankind has been fashioning quartz crystal into unique shapes for objects of beauty, service, magic and religious ritual. The hardness, permanence, durability, and beauty of rock crystal (along with its mystical properties) has ensured that this mineral will be revered throughout the ages.

The use of crystal as a tool of mind expansion has been recorded many times in history. In the King James version of the Bible, there are several references to the Urim and Thummim. Webster defines the Urim and Thummim as "certain objects mentioned in the Old Testament as being mediums for the revelaton of the will of God to his people or as being placed in the breastplate by the High Priest on certain occasions."

These two objects were believed by many Bible scholars to be quartz crystal. One was a smoky dark color, the other a light clear crystal. They represented opposites: day and night, yes and no, up and down. In this form of lot casting or drawing, the two crystals could answer any question of opposites. That is, guilty or innocent, left or right, good or bad, etc. It was an oracular device, a means by which Yahweh could be consulted.

In Exod. 28, Moses on the Mount of Sinai receives the instructions for the Tabernacle and is told that Aaron and his sons are to minister in the priest's office. Their garments and accouterments are described, "and thou shalt put in the breastplate of judgment one Urim and Thummim; and they shall be upon Aaron's heart when he goeth in before the Lord; and Aaron shall bear the judgment of the children of Israel upon his heart before the Lord continually."

In Lev. 8:9, Moses consecrates Aaron and his sons, saying: "This is the thing which the Lord commanded to be done." They are washed and robed, and "He put the breastplate upon him; also he put in the breastplate the Urim and Thummim." In Deut. 33:8, Moses, blessing Israel before his death: "And of Levi he said let thy Urim and Thummim be with the holy one."

In I Sam. 5 and 6, "And when Saul saw the host of the Philistines, he was afraid and his heart greatly trembled. And when Saul enquired of the Lord, the Lord answered him not, neither by dreams, nor by Urim nor by prophets." In Ezra 2:63, a cultic problem is postponed until a priest can consult the Urim and Thummim. "And Tirshatha said unto them, that they should not eat of the most holy things, till there stood up a priest with the Urim and Thummim." Neh. 7:65 is identical to this.

In Num. 27, Moses asks God to appoint his successor, and the Lord said to take Joshua. Verse 21 states: "He shall stand before Eleazar the priest who shall ask counsel for him after the judgment of Urim and Thummim before the Lord." There are other references where Yahweh was consulted in the same manner, very likely using the Urim and Thummim, but these will serve to make the point that these stones were important.

McKenzie's *Dictionary of the Bible* states that later the priests wore the Urim and Thummim only as decorations, that they were an extremely primitive device for ascertaining the will of the Deity. It is easy to see that this type of judgment could have been polluted by dishonesty.

It is believed that the adepts of ancient times fully understood the mystical feedback that occurs with rock quartz crystal. The knowledge was never really lost, but was a closely guarded secret held only by a special few. It was not by chance that the Crystal Skull was fashioned from crystal.

From earliest times is found a connection between crystal and esoteric religious practices. There are examples still standing today of churches built during the Middle Ages where crystal was used to inlay the altars. There is every reason to believe this practice originated with much earlier civilizations. The most sacred part of the church, the altar, was usually inlaid with seven (the mystical number) of stones. This is repeated in church altars in many parts of the world.

The first stone was a large rock quartz crystal. It was often called a diamond, but it was actually a clear, colorless crystal. The clear quartz represented strength. The second stone was blue sapphire for wisdom. The third stone, a green emerald, was often of green quartz crystal. This stood for adaptability. Fourth was the topaz, a yellow quartz crystal, citrine, for knowledge. The jaspar was fifth, for beauty. The sixth, a red ruby, for devotion. Seventh was the amethyst, also a crystal, for adoration and prayer.

It is interesting to note that four out of the seven (more than half) were usually quartz crystal, especially if they were of any great size. A true emerald is very small, but green quartz can be found in massive chunks.

During the rule of the Emperor Tiberius, who ruled 14 A.D. to 37 A.D., a man by the name of Appolonius was born in Tyana, Cappadocia, now a part of Turkey. Legend has it that he lived to be 100 years old, living until the reign of Nerva, 96-98 A.D. Appolonius is reported to have directed the first scientific survey of the world, sending expeditions to the coast of South America.

Historians have not dealt kindly with Appolonius. He became known as a sorcerer and a magician. However, it is a matter of record that he went to India and studied with the holy men of Kashmir. A vegetarian, he refused to wear clothing made from animal skins, for he did not believe in animal sacrifice. He understood the teachings of Pythagoras.

He was summoned before Caesar Dominicus to stand trial for sorcery and meddling with the spirits. Although he was a great distance away, he materialized in front of the Emperor. He was tried and found guilty, but he dematerialized and reappeared again shortly afterward near distant Mt. Vesuvius. Appolonius understood and used a quartz crystal. Apparently this famous first-century mystic held the secret of the remarkable property of quartz crystal to make opaque objects invisible.

A modern Viennese scientist maintained that the secret lay in the manner in which the stone was cut. He believed that when cut to a certain angle, exposed to sunlight, then placed in the mouth, the intoning of a certain magical incantation would cause the body to become invisible.

Unfortunately, the magical formula has been lost. Possibly Appolonius held the key to the knowledge of how the huge stones were moved to build the pyramids and Stonehenge.

Esoterically it is said that Stonehenge was designed to be built of crystal. Unfortunately only crystal-bearing rock was used. The standing stones in England and Scotland, the *menhires*, are crystalline and were cut to certain proportions to effect a certain resonance. This understanding, too, has been lost.

In Celtic literature, Merlin was said to have

full command of the power generated in the Crystal Cave and to have used this power to put Arthur on the throne of England. The Druids carried a crystal as a symbol of their spiritual power. The Chinese called the quartz crystal the *living stone*. The Vikings used crystal as an aid in navigation. The Minoans watched their captives from Crete perform with the bulls in the ring through quartz crystal magnifying lens. The crystal would give them a close-up view of the arena, while they sat safely high in box seats.

The Egyptians had smoky quartz sunglasses. Though at times referred to as emeralds, these were undoubtedly green quartz, as emeralds have never been found in large sizes. They also used crystal in their sacred ceremony to open the third eye of the dead.

In one of the last steps in mummification, a quartz crystal was placed on the brow of the deceased before the mummy was wrapped in the ceremonial cloths, which were dipped in spices and waxes and asphaltum. The crystal was placed in the position of the third eye, so the person could then look into the wonders and splendors of the heavens as they journeyed in the spirit world.

A rock quartz crystal was always placed in the west wall of a pyramid for protection (where, it was believed, all evil came).

From one of the Vedas of ancient India, writings some 7,000 years old, comes this poem:

INDRA'S NET

There is an endless net of threads throughout the Universe.

The horizontal threads are in space; the vertical threads in time.

At every crossing of threads there is an individual, and every individual is a crystal bead.

The great light of Absolute Being illuminates and penetrates every crystal bead.

And also, every crystal bead reflects not only the light from every other crystal in the net,

But also every reflection of every reflection throughout the Universe.

A Latin epic poet, named Claudianus (365 A.D. - 408 A.D.), wrote an illuminating and very revealing impression of crystal:

Pass not the shapeless lump of crystal by,
Nor view the icy mass with careless eye.
All royal pomp its value far exceeds,
And all the pearls the Red Sea's bosom breeds.
This rough and unformed stone, without a grace,
Mid'st rarest treasures, holds the chiefest place.

Obviously, from the above lines, Claudianus was aware that there existed a deeper spiritual and mental value to crystal than that expressed in the marketplace.

The goddess Asteria (for whom the asterisk is named) was the protectoress of crystal. Mother Earth and Father Sky mated and their offspring were called Titans. Asteria was the daughter of Koios and Phoibe. Titan means "nature power" and Phoibe means "bright and of the moon." The ancient sages worked only under certain signs of the Moon, using crystal and silver, both of which are symbols of the Moon. The goddess Asteria married Perseus and produced a child, Hekate. Asteria, the benevolent goddess of all the mysteries, taught her daughter all that she knew. The goddess Hekate used the knowledge for her own power and became the Queen of Hell, patron saint of witches.

However, this Hell was not the place of everlasting fire, as the Christian version is. Hekate presided over a place where souls, too out of harmony to advance to higher realms, could go to be healed. Since no soul is ever lost, or refused another chance to remake its life, the Hell of Hekate provided a resting place. The soul was cleansed, revitalized, reconditioned, and made to forget all the terrible things that had happened to it. Hekate's Hell was a training ground where souls could be cared for until they were ready to return to the world, either through reincarnation or in spirit form.

Asteria directs and channels crystal energies into higher levels of consciousness and higher astral levels of awareness for those who work for the betterment of their fellow man. Her message for mankind is that the bounty of the universe is man's rightful heritage. To confuse poverty with spirituality is wrong. Abundance is humankind's right, but it must be in a flow-through pattern. Hoarding is a wrong equal to poverty. The greatest blessing man can receive is to work with the natural flow of energies throughout the world, both receiving and giving, in prodigious amounts. This is true of any wealth, be it food, precious jewels, money , land, or whatever.

ASTERIA

Asteria! Starry One!
Bestow wisdom on daughter and son.
Holy water turned to stone
The power of crystal now is known.

All hail, Mother of Hekate!
As given to her, bequeath to me:
Knowledge, love, generosity.
Initiate me in the mysteries!

A. Bryant

Chapter Ten

PROPERTIES OF QUARTZ CRYSTAL

What is it about quartz crystal that makes it so special? Why would craftsmen from unnamed ancient civilizations choose to carve important objects in crystal?

To be sure, quartz crystal is very beautiful. Because of its extreme hardness it is very durable. Quartz crystal is ageless. Yet there is another reason why sculptors, even working with primitive tools, would seek to carve lasting objects of art from quartz crystal. That is because of its mystical, seemingly magical properties of how it interacts with the mind—almost as if it were a living stone.

It is not completely understood how the measurable electricity of the brain waves affects the vibrations of crystal. We do know that crystal is the only known substance that responds to energies broadcast by the conscious and subconscious mind. It is safe to assume that future developments will show that there are others.

The biofeedback instruments are just one example of the possible developments in this field. In crystal, there is a reaction when you come close enough for it to be in the energy field (magnetic field or aura) of your body. That is, crystal has its own vibration, but being touched by a human being changes its vibrations so that they are in harmony with those of the person holding it.

Experiments have shown that it will not respond greatly to a person sitting three feet away; but paradoxically, a crystal on a table surrounded by four people does respond. It responds, not with four times the power, but with about sixteen times the power.

This can be compared to the center armature on an electric motor, with the people corresponding to the field wirings. With eight or ten people, the power increases according to the same ratio. One person working with a crystal must hold it or be within two or three feet of it for the crystal to pick up the energy. Any piece of crystal is just that, a piece of crystal, regardless of the shape (crystal ball, talisman, meditation piece), until it is energized by a person. Otherwise, it is just like a radio that is not switched on. The radio waves are still active, but nothing is received.

The object is to reach beyond the five conscious senses, to channel the energies to extend into the invisible world, which also runs on electrical energy. Studies indicate that the entire Universe is actually nothing but electrical energy with positive and negative force fields. The most minute subatomic particle is composed of electrical energy in a constant state of motion or vibration. Our eyes can see only certain wavelengths and vibrations.

Madame Marie Curie ushered in the Age of Aquarius with her research on the ability of quartz crystal to oscillate. This occurred in 1889 with her experimentation and use of piezoelectric quartz crystal to classify emission rays of radium. It was due to these early findings that our present civilization could advance so rapidly with the aid of radio, TV, telephones, satellites, and moon shots. All of these derived from the basic knowledge of how to control wavelengths of motion. The Age of Aquarius is known scientifically as the Crystal Age, the mineral symbol of Aquarius being quartz crystal. This is the age of advanced communications, and most of our modern communications systems are based on the crystal oscillators.

The reason you can tune a radio or a TV to a certain place on the dial is because the TV or radio station is broadcasting on an exact wavelength. It has a control mechanism, a quartz crystal oscillator, which oscillates at only so many thousand cycles per second and remains that way constantly. Therefore, you can tune in at, say, 1040 on the dial because of a little chip of quartz crystal oscillating at an exact frequency that does not vary.

In natural quartz crystal, only the top part—where it is an absolutely clear, impurity-free, single crystal—is the electronic part. Scientists discovered that if you take pure electronic crystal and imbed an impurity in it, such as iron oxide or some other element, it will differ from a pure one and will react differently under electronic use. "Solid state" in radio or TV means there are no tubes. The tubes are replaced by solid-state transistors. These transistors are active semi-conductor devices usually made of silicon or germanium.

This breakthrough came from the knowledge that crystals with certain impurities imbedded within them differed from other crystals because of the impurity content and not the purity. This allows "crystals," or the modern transistor, to be manufactured to fit certain needs.

How Quartz Crystal Is Formed

Natural quartz crystal is produced by tremendous heat and pressure. This can be supplied by an earthquake or a volcano. When natural crystal is exposed to radiation, such as that which occurs naturally in many places in the Earth's crust, the radiation gradually displaces an electron in each atom. This results in the crystal changing from pure white to various shades of colors. It can become all the various shades of amethyst, varying from light smoke to a deep, mysterious, transparent black. When chemical impurities are present, these tint the crystal in many shades of yellow, rose, blue, and green. It can also be said that crystal endures forever, because it neither ages, oxidizes, nor decays. It is so hard that wear is seldom seen. It is so pure that scientists use it for the contamination-free test tubes in which radioactive carbon age dating is done.

One of the unusual properties of crystal not clearly understood is the crystal seed. Any piece of natural quartz crystal can be a seed. Quartz crystal will dissolve in water under intense heat and pressure. The liquid crystal cells appear to have a "memory" that makes them seek out any nearby existing crystal to attach themselves to, thus building a new, perfect, latticework crystal structure.

Even as a tomato seed needs nutrients such as water and sunshine or warmth to grow, so a crystal seed will not grow without a nutrient. This nutrient is silicon dioxide. The combination of pressure from an earthquake and heat produced by volcanic rupture of the Earth's crust will cause the seed to grow. It grows rapidly, like a spiral staircase, growing either right- or left-handed, clockwise or counterclockwise. This is not visible to the naked eye, for a crystal has smooth sides.

When a crystal is submerged in a tank containing a liquid of the same refraction index as the crystal, and a polarized light is passed through it and then observed through a polarized screen, the crystal will show a sequence of colors ranging from red to yellow to blue, similar to a rainbow.

As the analyzer is turned clockwise by an observer, the rings expand in a right-hand crystal and contract in a left-hand crystal. The Crystal Skull is a left-hand crystal.

Because high quality crystal is in short supply, crystal is grown in labs today. The high-tech electronic company, Hewlett-Packard, and many other electronic companies, are growing their own crystals.

Using a tiny "seed," a crystal as large as a building brick can be grown in 30 to 45 days in the following manner: A large steel case, very heavy and thick, with a top that will unscrew, is partially filled with silicon dioxide in the form of pieces of pure quartz crystal. These tiny scrap chunks of natural quartz crystal contain all the elements necessary for growing a large crystal. The rest of the space is filled with mineralized water and the seed crystal is suspended above the scrap crystal feedstock with a tiny wire. With the top of the container tightly closed, the steel case is lowered into a vault. This vault, usually subterranean, has a hatch similar to a submarine hatch that closes and seals.

The container is electrically heated to an intense temperature, resulting in tremendous pressures inside the sealed chamber. The crystal scraps dissolve and the liquid crystal cells migrate, attaching themselves uniformly and in perfect building patterns to the mother seed crystal. After the optimum time has elapsed (a matter of weeks), the heat is turned off and the entire area is left to cool slowly. Although there are some carefully guarded trade secrets, that is the general method used. Thousands of pounds of lab-grown crystals are used every year in the electronic trade.

As an excellent example of recycling, not only clear electronic crystals are produced but also, by carefully controlled additives to the water, select quality amethyst, citrine, blue, green and smoke crystals are obtained. Crystals are being grown in several countries: the United States, Germany, France, Japan, and Russia are large producers at this time.

The grown crystals may be compared to a hothouse tomato which is grown under controlled conditions so that the end result is superior in size and color and taste. It is still a tomato, but it is better in every sense because all of its needs are met at the right time and the handicaps to its growth are minimized. Grown crystals, since the needs are supplied in a controlled environment, grow very rapidly and their structure and quality are excellent.

A crystal grows in a hexagonal shape; i.e.: six-sided, from a matrix up to a point. The lengthwise part is called the C axis. On any one of the six flat sides, looking directly into the flat side, is the Y axis. This axis is referred to as the mechanical side. The electrical axis, or X axis, is found on any one of the sharp corners, looking directly at one of the sharp edges.

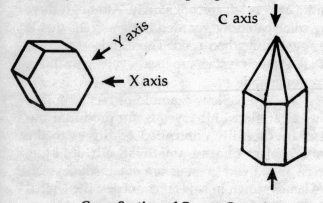

Cross Section of Quartz Crystal

Originally, manufactured crystals had a drawback as far as commercial use was concerned. Using what was termed second and third generation crystals, the error ratio could be as great as four or five times. Where natural crystal (perhaps 300,000 years old) that was ground into an oscillator and used on a frequency of 2000 cycles per second would not vary, a brand-new manufactured crystal could vary from 1993 cycles to 2006 cycles per second. The variation was not important if the crystal was used for watches, telephone equipment, radios, or hi-fi equipment. It would have been a serious deficiency in a computer used for space exploration. Due to improved technology, grown crystals are now superior electronically in every way (with no error ratio) to all but the rarest natural crystals.

Crystal has become expensive, and all of it is now being utilized. Jewelry manufacturers grind it up, melt it, and pour it into huge slabs. These can be sliced, much as one slices a loaf of bread. This crystal is excellent for telescopic lenses, optical lenses, and it makes beautiful jewelry. Crystal handled in this manner does not lose its beauty, gloss, or refractive index. It does lose all its electronic properties. It is only the pure natural-state quartz crystal that will respond to human vibrations.

The electronic part of a crystal is the top part where it is pure and one single crystal. The bottom part where it grows out of the matrix is much less so. Pure quartz crystal can contain veils, feathers, and inclusions that are very beautiful. While these imperfections make it unsuitable for electronic use, they do not affect the crystal's ability to become energized by an individual.

Lead Crystal
Man-made crystal with a lead content will not respond to human vibrations. Lead crystal is

more like a shield and insulator, for lead is used for protection from x-rays. The term "crystal" does not necessarily mean natural quartz crystal; it can mean lead crystal. Crystal that has been melted down, purified, cast, and polished is still 100 per cent quartz crystal, but the processing has destroyed the unique latticework structure so that it no longer has any reaction capabilities. It is dead. It is the electronic part of crystal that has a vibratory response to energy, whether this energy is from batteries, electric power lines, or a human being.

The supply of good crystals in the world today is becoming limited, and more people are turning to the crystals grown in laboratories. There is no objection to using a crystal that is artificially grown, because both the nutrient ingredients and the electronic properties are the same as natural crystal.

Basically, crystals are tools, as plants for food are tools. Whether grown in the ground or grown in a lab, the crystal is a tool that can assist one's creativity, and once recognized as such, can make the creativity flow easier and smoother.

One must have a body to experience physical reality. One must breathe air, which is a tool, and clothe the body and feed it by using tools. The crystal is a tool to use to gain a greater level of creativity. If a carpenter who used a rock for a hammer invented a metal hammer, he would be using his creativity to put his energy to a better and more efficient use. So crystals, used with that potential in mind, give a greater freedom in the levels of creativity. They do not *cause* the freedom, they stimulate the inner knowledge of that freedom, its ready availability, its power and strength.

Single Terminated Quartz Crystal

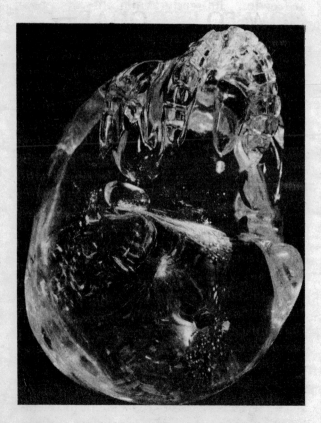

Partial right side and underneath view showing ground prisms in Crystal Skull

Chapter Eleven

HOW TO USE QUARTZ CRYSTAL

To energize and be energized by your crystal, you need to focus your own electrical field in one direction. A study done at Loma Linda College in California has shown that the two halves of the brain are seldom in synchronization. Since the two halves, the creative and the logical, do not automatically synchronize, it is necessary to put them in harmony. This is done by reaching a deep meditative state, and synchronicity may be one explanation as to why these deep levels of mind are so powerful. This state is reached by relaxation. Focusing on an object, such as a candle or a flower, can be helpful to stop the mind from darting off in distracting directions.

The crystal can be of great benefit for meditating and reaching that quiet, inner state of peace where the answers to all questions can be found.

Having chosen a crystal that feels right for you—and here size is not a factor, though a good choice is one that fits comfortably in the palm of the hand—program your crystal by holding it, stroking it, and speaking aloud to it.

Practice enables you to go to the perfect level instantly when you pick up your crystal and choose to do so. It takes practice to get to the perfect level for what you are seeking—problem-solving, healing, self-healing, creativity, better understanding of people, situations, events. At this level you can tap into abilities that are unavailable at other levels.

At times in these deeper levels of mind you may see only beautiful colors. It is not unusual to feel that nothing happened. Then the answers will pop into your mind when you are busy at something else. For some, the colors are replaced with symbols, and it is necessary to ask your mind to interpret them for you. Others hear a voice within, or a picture is formed in the inner vision.

This is why crystal is so valuable. It is the tool by which we enhance our inherent abilities. The crystal must be *your* crystal. You must work with it, interact with its energies.

These deeper levels of mind are multidimensional. In expanding our awareness inwardly toward our Source, we are activating pathways in heretofore unused portions of the mind/brain.

Your crystal, in strengthening and reinforcing your power, sharpens your ability to visualize, and visualization is one of the most important methods to be used in establishing contact with the Universal Mind. The subconscious cannot tell the difference between what is vividly imagined to be true and what is reality. If you visualize a desired end result, the mind is then put into operation to attract, obtain, and achieve that particular visualization.

The mind needs to be trained in visualization, for often we do not understand how to ask the right questions. How can you know it is communication with the Universal Mind? If it is a quantum leap away from your ordinary thinking, when it is creative, solves a problem, answers a question, and is not logically arrived at step by step but is a new thought, then it is from the Universal Mind. It will always be satisfying and right for everyone concerned. If it is troublesome, irritating, unsatisfying, then it is your ego, so return to the meditative state and try again!

For some, the idea that they can be in contact with the Universal Mind, Supreme Intelligence, God, Goddess, All That Is, is incredible, if not downright terrifying. If you have that reaction, try to think back to when you were told you could not do so. Try to remember when, as a child, you did not differentiate as to *how* you learned things. You just absorbed them, you did not question the source. Jesus, the Christ, said, "Unless ye become as a little child . . ."

The cells work together to form a body. When the body becomes ill, it is because the cell has ceased to do its task properly. It ceases to direct energy in the way that it should. The distortion can be corrected by refocusing the energy in the cell. When man understands that mind can control the mechanism by which a cell directs energy correctly, or in the case of disease, incorrectly, then all diseases will be cured. A crystal helps to amplify this energy at the cell level. Know that your thoughts direct the overall functioning of your body's cells, and that your thoughts create your reality. (For more information on crystal healing, see *Crystal Healing: The Next Step* by Phyllis Galde, Llewellyn Publications.)

The use of color is very beneficial in healing. Choose a color that feels like a healing color to you. Feel it flowing over you, penetrating your body. You do not make the healing happen, you *allow* it to happen. Our problems are for the most part caused by blocking the healing process by tension, erroneous ideas, wrong programming. Healing is normal and natural, not magic. It is part of our heritage, our original equipment that we have allowed to fade.

Scientifically, the value of the crystal lies in the transmission of radio amplification. A hand-held crystal receives the impulses and the energy from the person who activates it. It receives all the different wavelengths broadcast from the subconscious and the higher conscious mind. Even the body cells are sending forth an electrical impulse. These are all amplified by the crystal, as in an amplifying reflector, then rebroadcast so that they are received into the conscious mind. The individual then begins to understand on a conscious level what was before only in the subconscious or stored in the body cells.

Cells have their own memories, and each cell remembers its past though all of its parts have been, and are, continually being replaced. All body cells are in a state of communication between themselves, the brain/mind, subconscious mind, higher conscious mind. There is a communication network in the body run by electronic energy.

The crystal is an electronic device constantly receiving and broadcasting these waves of information. Thus, color means nothing scientifically, for the radio waves have nothing to do with color, but people *perceive* colors in different ways. Individuals have different likes and dislikes, different feelings and meanings for colors. The color of a crystal is extremely important to some individuals, for colors are symbols to the mind, and the mind *does* care.

We have been programmed to believe that certain colors mean certain things. From its memory bank, its mental conditioning, pre-training, pre-programming, the mind understands that, for instance, blue is the color of peace, red of vigor, green of springtime/growth. Color is even more important to users of crystal, because they are using their inner senses.

Colors of Quartz Crystal

Crystal can be found in all colors. The most common is clear rock quartz. Smoky quartz ranges from a deep, dense, almost black (known as a Scottish crystal called *caringorm,*) into warm rich browns, cold browns, to lighter browns. There is champagne quartz which ranges from a pale, straw color to lemon yellow, to citrine, to a deep topaz. Though it is seldom mentioned in print, there is a beautiful red and there is a green smoke. The blue crystals are very rare and small. However, recycled or laboratory-grown crystals are available in beautiful blues.

Crystals that have been recycled can have different colors. The recycling laboratories are refining tiny crystals into one large crystal, losing the impurities in the process. There are millions of tons of tiny, real crystals full of impurities and flaws that are too small to be cut which can be used for feed stock. Dissolved and re-grown on the seed crystal, they are grown by nature, just as if it had taken hundreds of thousands of years. They are not substitutes. They are the real thing, only scientifically grown, and they are then free from impurities.

Manufacturers are making artificial rubies

and emeralds. For people who find significance in color, the metaphysicians, there is a need for all colors that work with the mind. There is a need for colors such as royal violet/pale blues and deeper blues/blue-greens/yellow-greens. This is possible now, but it is not being done. We will at some time have clear, beautiful golden yellows such as the world has never seen. There will be blues, violets, and amethysts that are spectacular and gorgeous. There will be healing greens that are so good for the soul. And, they will enrich the world.

Colored Quartz and the Chakras

The colors of crystals are grouped into three groups that correspond with the chakras. Each color is a specific vibration and each differs from the other. The variations of red, orange, and yellow pertain to creation, the lower three chakras, the emotional planes. Green, blue and purple are connected with the higher chakras, with green and blue applying to the mental. For the highest chakras, use the crystals with the pale yellow, golden touches and the clear ones with silver glints. Lavender and clear with silver and gold apply to the spiritual chakras. A smoky quartz crystal with golden tints can, when one's consciousness is focused into it, take one to higher levels, to information points where one can achieve an information exchange, not as a memory bank or a library, but as a vibrant, alive exchange of knowledge.

Using Your Crystals Effectively

It is important to imprint your crystals with your goals. Until you know what you want, it is difficult, if not impossible, to achieve anything. Goals should be set for short term, intermediate, and long term. The short-term goals are to be accomplished today, this week, this month. The intermediate goals are for periods up to six months. Long-term goals are plans for the future, for your life's work. They should be compatible, not diametrically opposed.

Talk to your crystal. The sound of your voice energizes it. How do you know it is your crystal? It will find you. Own one, use it, and you will soon find yourself owning a family of crystals. They call to you.

Price is not a true criteria of value, nor is clarity versus cloudiness. Crystals with a high, true, energy pattern can only be detected by feel. As you learn to work with crystals and come to understand them, they will feel different to you. Offer someone new to crystals a choice of half a dozen or so. It may take them awhile, but after handling them, they can quite happily choose one that is for them.

The ultraviolet rays of the Sun have an effect on crystal. After being placed in the Sun for a short time, it can be reprogrammed with sound. As you purify the crystal, you can transfer the concept of purification to yourself, using a visual concept of cleansing and renewal brought within, from the pure Cosmic energy. In this process you become one with your surroundings and one with the crystal.

Since man has created his own illusion, he has also created the standard and the formula for disillusion. When he can step through the illusion and into another level of creativity, the process becomes simplified. When the consciousness can be raised or expanded to a point, it is possible to blend with all vibrations that come into contact with the crystal, not being changed or dispelled, but blending, as with the Universal Source. The illusion is in seeing things as limited; they are unlimited. The limitation is in the appearance which is temporary. The Cosmic Force is permanent and underlies everything. The entire existence of material things is based on illusion, and when one touches reality, illusion vanishes, for reality is stronger.

If you hold a crystal and focus your energy, you can either focus on the outside of the surface of the crystal, no matter what the shape, or you can focus in the very center. On the surface you deal with the lower vibrations; with the center you deal with the higher ones. The energies of the crystals that are man-made are locked into the Earth plane, they affect the physical phenomena of this planet.

We are turning more and more toward

holistic thinking—that wo/man is a spirit and has a body and that the two are intricately connected, not separate.

If mental healing is mind affecting energy which in turn affects matter, then a major part of mental healing is the transfer of energy. The concentration of one's mind increases the incoming energy and transfers it to the person in need, who, in turn, uses it to heal him/herself.

A crystal focuses the mind, and when the energy of the mind goes in and comes out it generates spirals of energy. As man grows and expands his consciousness, his attention is less in the physical focus and more out in an expanded view of the spiritual focus and of all creation. Many ancient peoples—the Amerindians, Tibetans, Mongolians—believed that in using crystal, if they could get the spiritual body healed and balanced, the physical body would copy or imitate the spiritual body

In ancient times there were those people who used the crystals and really understood them. They used them as tools. And then there were those who did *not* understand them, but realized that their psychic abilities were enhanced when using crystals. Those that wanted to have psychic abilites ground the crystals so that they could amplify or diminish the powers of the stone. Thus we find crystals that have been ground with a concave or a convex side, which would magnify their powers somewhat. Man had learned that crystal was a way to help movement of energy and focus it.

It is believed that in a space and time where crystals were in use, it was found that by cutting the clear ones in very thin pieces, the crystals could be moved by mind energy. This was done when it was dark outside, not during the day, because when the mind has less stimulation from light it can focus easier. The crystals are easier to work with if one does not visually put one's energy into them.

All civilizations have had a concept of a Supreme Deity. Whether the name was God, Cosmic Consciousness, Universal Mind, Buddha, Enlightened One, Krishna, Ometeotl, Quetzalcoatl, or Zeus, the name is immaterial. It is the *idea* that is important. And, the idea is in the MIND. One can only "know" a higher power through one's thoughts and emotions. Without his mind, man is less than the animals. With the powers of the mind, man can be on a level with the angels. This "knowing" can be achieved without a crystal, certainly, but *with* the use of a crystal, all capabilities are amplified.

Always when a civilization falls, much is lost. The Old World's knowledge suffered from the burning of the library at Alexandria. In the New World, the Spaniards, with their greed and rapacity, seeking only gold, destroyed a far greater treasure. Montezuma was unresisting, because he was paralyzed by the old prophecies: "Thirteen Heavens of decreasing choice, Nine Hells of increasing doom."

Cortez arrived at Veracruz in 1519, the year Ce Acatl (One Reed) by the Sacred Calendar, the day prophesied for the return of Quetzalcoatl. But for the Aztecs, it was not the benevolent Quetzalcoatl, father and creator, but rather, the twin brother, Xolotl, he of the fleshless skull. Time for the Aztecs had run out. Their world, as they knew it, would be no more.

The ticking of the Cosmic Clock did not stop simply because those who understood it best no longer marked the passing of the days. The Fifth World would end, the Sixth World begin. More precisely, the calculations that have been checked through two computer banks say that the Cosmic Clock ticked off the end of the Fifth World on August 17, 1987, thus marking the Harmonic Convergence and the 25-year countdown to the beginning of the New Age, 2212 A.D.

Our distant ancestors wished to bequeath a most important message. The vehicle they chose was a sculptured rendition in quartz crystal, a skull as reminder of the repository of the mind and soul. It is the outer covering of the aware- ness part of man. A fleshless head to symbolize all of the human race, for it is completely free from any restrictions of race, color, or creed. It is not black, white, brown, or yellow. It is not a symbol of any religion or belief. It is the endur- ing symbol of the essence of man, his durability, his purity and above all his potential. For it is through the *mind* of man that his heights and his depths, his successes and his failures are manifested.

Quartz crystal neither changes with age nor decays. The crystal would carry the legacy forward over eons of time—the symbol of the divine gift of immortality, freedom of choice, the eternal progress of the human soul. The single cell from which we sprang threads itself back to the dawn of time. Each individual is important, having taken so long to be perfected.

It is an unacceptable premise that any soul could be doomed to annihilation after merely visiting for a short time on planet Earth.

Kahil Gibran said it well in *The Prophet*:

"When you were a silent word upon Life's quivering lips, I too, was there, another silent word. Then Life uttered us and we came down the years throbbing with memories of yesterday and with longing for tomorrow, for yesterday was death conquered and tomorrow was birth pursued."

View of M-H Crystal Skull from the top. Eye sockets visible in front (top). Natural prism can be seen in middle. Under back, holes for manipulating rods to animate Skull can be seen.

Part Two:

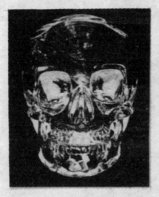

The Psychic Speculation

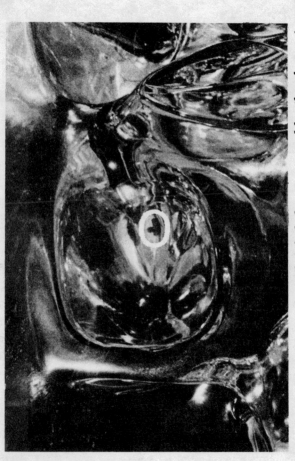

Enlargement of right eye socket. The circled scene resembles the observatory at the Chichen Itza Mayan ruins.

Chapter Twelve

PSYCHIC SPECULATION ABOUT THE CRYSTAL SKULL

Introduction

After the Dorlands came to understand the reaction of crystal to human energies, it became more and more apparent that the Crystal Skull had a far deeper meaning than a work of art or even as an object of worship. Any piece of crystal of that size would interact with human energies with tremendous force. Obviously the carving of the Crystal Skull indicated that the makers were aware of the power of crystal.

In seeking help in their scientific studies from the universities and knowledgeable people, the Dorlands hit an absolute dead end. Research in the libraries proved to be of limited value.

The Dorlands had proved that the Crystal Skull was not a fake. It was legitimate, extremely rare, and probably very ancient. But, it had no written history. Being deeply religious, they turned to the Source—within.

The following excerpts are from more than one channel. They were arrived at through an altered state of consciousness. They are offered without comment for the readers to draw their own conclusions.

[Each psychic approaches the Crystal Skull from a different angle. Rather than seeing them as being in conflict, look at it from the interesting perspective that all have a unique pattern of information to share.]

Rev. Peggy Kahn

Rev. Peggy Kahn was born in Manchester, England. She graduated from Bristol University just prior to WW II. During the war years, she worked for the British Admiralty. In 1946, she married an American and moved to Pennsylvania. After her three children were grown, she began a full-time career in metaphysics and pyschic studies. She has lectured from coast to coast and at the Arthur Findlay Spiritual College in England. She has served as spiritual advisor in Pennsylvania, Arizona and California. She served for four years as pastor at the historical Church of the Comforter in Santa Barbara, CA.

As the Piscean Age closes and the Aquarian Age begins, we have to realize that no age closes without a general housecleaning. In the last 100 to 150 years we have been making strange discoveries in religious points of history across the globe, bringing to life clarifications and explanations, and even confirmations of certain truths, that have not always been accepted by the orthodox religions. As we come to the end of the Piscean Age into the Aquarian Age, we are clearing up odds and ends. We are moving into the Crystal Age, the Aquarian Age, with its symbol of water dropping from an urn. Why water when Aquarius is an air sign? We are speaking of vibrations of mentality, not just air in the sense of wind blowing from pole to pole.

The Aquarian Age, the age of crystals, can be translated metaphysically as symbolic of droplets of high mental and spiritual thoughts descending to the physical plane. We are moving through changing vibrations, as we do in each astrological cycle, not only in our lifetime but in the lifetimes of the planet. Thus the finding of the Crystal Skull becomes more than just an archaeological find—a precious jewel—it is a symbolic treasure heralding the emergence of crystal into the conscious mind of modern man.

It does not matter how it was found, or where. The important fact is that it was found at all, at the closing of an age. It was the emerging of crystal into the conscious mind of modern-day man.

As this planet is moving back into the Aquarian Age, mankind cannot leap from the vibrations of Piscean thinking directly into the understanding of the Aquarian Age without having some link between the two. Crystal is the visible, tangible link to be used as a bridge between the two levels of consciousness. That is what the two ages symbolize, a changing level of consciousness from the old to the new. That is the importance of crystal. Crystal will be used for many, many other things than man has yet devised, for the Aquarian Age is the age of communication. It would be interesting to know if the records that speak of the shamans having a piece of crystal placed under the skin, sewn into the body itself, then transferred from one to another, as one died, if that was done during an Aquarian Age. The stories, no matter when they were written, were speaking of a use of, and an understanding of, crystal being used to bridge the gap between changing vibrations.

Without a doubt the Crystal Skull had to have been a very powerful, well-understood, and knowledgeably used instrument of vibration for higher spiritual understanding in an age that was Aquarian. It would be interesting to know if the emergence of the Crystal Skull, possibly from the times of Atlantis, has been in Aquarian Ages.

We are today what we have been in a past life. We are today sowing the seeds of what we will be in the future. The choice to further our evolvement, to polish the facets of the soul, is ours to make. Crystal is one of the best tools to help one contact the unconscious part of his programming, his memory bank. This contact assists one to understand why one behaves the way one does in certain circumstances. Understanding them, one can then reprogram and direct one's future, free of earlier influences.

There are rays, not new, of cosmic energy that have not in the past astrological ages been bombarding this planet, but that are doing so now. Not only do we need crystal as a stimulator to form the vibration bridge between the two ages, but we are going to need crystal as a degree of protection, a filtering.

It is going to be very difficult for the gross matter of humanity, mankind, to respond to these changing vibrations without having some pure substance, and crystal is a pure substance, through which to filter these energies coming from the cosmic areas and now bombarding the Earth. We cannot yet sustain them in their full force. Crystal helps to disburse, to channel these energies.

The Crystal Skull disappears and reappears over thousands of years in accordance with changing cycles of awareness. Those who first created it (to us a great engineering masterpiece inconceivable in its execution—but it may have not been difficult for them), to those who made it, it must have had great spiritual significance. Surely the spiritual artifacts throughout history have not been lost by man's carelessness, but rather through catastrophic geographic occurrences. It is not man that has kept it hidden, but a certain Divine Order, for its purpose and vibrational use within a certain age.

In meditation I was shown a large inner chamber. It seemed to be hewn within a side of a cliff, at an angle going down into the Earth. With great reverence and ceremony, the Crystal Skull was placed in the center of a room that appeared illuminated without any light source. The Elders were gathered around the Crystal Skull, receiving as mental telepathy, rather than verbal communication, emanations as they seemed to rise from the Skull. There seemed to be a signal at one point for everyone to leave. I was given the impression that those who were there, who had used the vibrations of the Skull in a spiritual sense, were saying goodby, because being one of the ones who moved away from this deep chamber, with such sorrow, I turned my back on the Crystal Skull and walked away.

The next picture shown, after some certain time that was not given, was of a great eruption and collapsing of a mountain, a collapsing of the material into the hidden room where those of us who had been part of this great ceremony had been gathered.

There followed, again without any time span indicated, a period when I was shown a golden man, a man so tall as to be 7' or 7'6", perfectly proportioned, with beautiful skin tones of a glorious bronze. The deep violet eyes seemed to have a sparkling light in them. He was dressed in a short tunic that was not out of place on him. The webbing of his belt seemed to be a soft metallic material. It looked like gold, gold or silver lamé metallic, yet soft and gentle.

This beautiful man was standing in a brilliant, extremely hot, tropical clime. He was reaching into a cavern, in which was discovered the Crystal Skull. He lifted it from its hiding place where apparently some earthquake or tremor had moved the rock and debris, bringing again to the surface the Crystal Skull for use in its right time. He took it with great ceremony up a long, very wide expanse of stairs that went, seemingly endlessly, toward the Heavens to what appeared to be a temple.

If we accept these visions of the history and beauty of the Crystal Skull, its meaning and purpose, it would seem there have been many men and women in many civilizations who have shared in its use. When the time, in prophecy, was due for them to leave and for the crystal to be hidden from the sight of man for a time, the farewells happened time and time again, and will continue to happen.

We are a part in consciousness of an Aquarian Age. Perhaps those who were before us did not realize the significance of their find, and looked upon it as an archeological wonder. Let us realize it is more than that. It is the symbol of our future, the symbol of our spirituality. Let it be used now, in the Aquarian Age, the Age of Crystal, for the betterment of mankind and for the betterment of the world at large.

Channeling from Frank Alper

Dr. Frank Alper is head of the Arizona Metaphysical Society. He is the author of Exploring Atlantis, *a trilogy of books dealing with ancient Atlantis and crystal healing. He is a conscious channel and is a pioneer in healing with magnetic energies using geometric configurations.*

Blessings to you. We are Adamis.

We are going to relate to you the reality of the presence of the crystal skulls upon the planet Earth. In totality, there were originally 22 that were created out of pure energy, and in one of your terms, apported to Earth. Several of them were brought by the ancient Lemurians, several brought by the Atlanteans, those who descended in the ships into the bowels of Earth to begin the reconstruction of these civilizations.

They were created as keepers of records. They contain energy patterns that record the history of the construction of your universe, and of descending hierarchal figures that faced the universe in Divine order.

The one that most of you have viewed this day was given to the ancient Mayans almost 1500 Earth years ago. Many souls incarnated in the ancient Mayan cultures were indeed service-oriented souls that had prior service in Lemuria and Atlantis.

. . . It was presented to them as a connecting link between the source of their souls and Love to remind them of their identity and to make available to them, when their consciousness became compatible, information that they could utilize in the proper construction and preservation of their civilization.

For example, to allow them to evolve proper methods of constructing the stone-lined channels as aquaducts for irrigation and waterways; the proper angles and construction of their homes, with openings placed in precise areas in relation to wind currents to allow for perfect circulation and temperature year round; and many other "tidbits" of information that helped them formulate their society and their methodology of existence.

The 22 skulls have been in various locations throughout this world. Each one has not been programmed in an identical manner, but programmed basically in relation to the souls incarnating in these areas pertaining to the future generations, of course. Out of the 22 there are only—to our recognition—12 remaining intact. The others have been destroyed by those who did not know what they had in their possession. One could safely say that within a period of 15 Earth years those that have not been uncovered shall be uncovered.

Can you imagine what would occur if all 12 of them were brought together and placed in one circle? It would be quite an exciting experience! Of course it could not be put on public display, for the majority of humans that would come to see them would literally go insane from the power of energy fields that would result in their generation.

· Utilized properly and on a one-to-one basis, not with such—I believe you call them "mobs"—they do indeed serve as initiation mediums for individuals. There is an instant mass opening of locked doors of recall and memory in one's mind.

The frequencies are of course totally magnetic in nature. They are not involved within God's love frequencies, although from time to time those of mankind who have touched the Skull have blessed it and placed to some small degree varying aspects of the love frequency. But the function was as a magnetic dispenser.

One who owns such a vehicle has a great obligation to the children of Light upon the planet Earth for its preservation and its well-being. Even though one owns it, they are merely the vehicle to expose it to all of the others who are to experience its energies, and never need to be concerned of negativity being implanted inside—the fields of vibration are too strong to permit this. It cannot enter. Besides, it is not receptive to that form of low frequency. The network of its polarized energies functions and operates totally within the magnetic fields. In this way, when the energy will be released, it shall be received and interpreted in total purity, without distortion.

There are other shaped objects also buried beneath the surface of Earth. There are 17 crystal obelisks, ranging in size from 20 inches to three of your feet in length, the greatest diameter being approximately eight of your inches. These obelisks were also created out of energy, transformed into physical matter of crystal.

These structures will help to prepare a stronger relation pertaining to the creation and inhabitation of your solar system, almost exclusively. None of these structures has been uncovered to this time, but this too shall come to pass.

The most important thing for you to understand and that shall benefit you from this experience today is that all knowledge—all knowledge—is present at any given time in energy form. It truly is not necessary, in order for one to learn, for one to be present inside of or to confront a physical object. Wherever you are, the information is available to you as long as you allow yourself and set the conditions of mind. One does not need a giant edifice to pray to God, to be in the house of the Lord, for the house is wherever you have created it in your mind.

And so this is another experience for you in learning to interpret and to find truth in areas beyond what seems to be. For at all times the total source of all that is your truth lies within the ethers. Many await you to connect yourself and bring down what is necessary into your conscious expressions.

The one who keeps this Skull at this time is truly a gentle soul, a true child of Light and of God. She is to be blessed for her attitude and for her service to God's children on Earth. May her light shine for many years to come. Our blessings to you.

Channeling from Lorraine Darr

Lorraine Darr is a gifted clairvoyant and trance medium. On countless occasions her accuracy and insights have helped many people through hurdles in their lives. Time and time again she has proven to be extremely accurate with her predictions. For the channeling which follows, she agreed to place herself into an unusually deep, complete trance for even greater clarity of answers.

In the name of the One and the mighty Three in One do I come and place this body for the purpose of bringing forth a clear understanding concerning the Crystal Skull. I call forth the Forms of Light which aided in the creation of the crystal skulls, and the Being of the crystal skulls themselves for the purpose of answering the questions Phyllis has prepared which will be part of a future work. I ask that the presence of the Ancient of Days be with me as these questions are answered and the Grand Mothers surround the allowing for truth and clarity. I know that Gabrielle abides in the process of information released, is watched over by Mark and John. Together, all of us here do rest in stillness for a clear transfer of knowledge and wisdom. We ask for watchful care over the physical body and other bodies by Mark and John while the teaching occurs. I know, image, and see for the many Forms in this clear allowing. So be it.

Transportation of that which you asked holds in the All, emanates from the Skull. The connection for this giving shall be with the Skull in the pictures, for this is perfected in its whole presentation as a form of sound. Now, within the Ages that this Skull participated upon this physical Earth, it was here in what you term land mass areas upon the Earth three times. With the third time that it came once again to the Earth, there was the decision that it should remain and connect fully with a duplicate skull, abiding in what you term other Spaces. The duplicate skull resides in what you know to be Sirius at this time. It has abided in what you know to be Arcturus and the Pleiades.

The purposes have been many, and we shall ask now for the flow of your askings, after which if there is yet information deemed useful to you in this time, it shall be given. Let us proceed.

Who first created the Crystal Skull?

This one created with streams of light from the hands of master craftsmen was accomplished in its Allness in what you term a neutral space. In other words, a group of Master Teachers gathered from the Planetary Council, abided in a mobile station, connected between the Sun and your Earth. Using pieces of crystal from various parts of what you term your physical Earth, there was the space of resonating the pieces to find those that would remain whole when the light was used from any direction. In that first creation, this Skull and another skull were done.

You need to see and recall that to have a large piece of crystal brought from a particular space filled with the energies of your Earth in that space, and in all spaces surrounding it, the purpose of creating the Skull was to use the Skull upon your land areas, within and for the development of races. In combination in a circle of ten there were what you would term Beings from the near worlds and the far worlds, the Suns, the Central Sun, the known planets, and specific star systems. Out of this group there were chosen ten Masters at the art of using the laser beam. Within this circle of ten, the first thing that was done was the agreed-upon image in all its perfection, held in the Mind. This was projected into the crystal piece. As it was held in a steady gaze, there were some small sounds, rather like a melting action. The lasers knew from the known design exactly what to do. The Masters completed the whole in what you could term three minutes.

Now, in the outer shape was there. The next part took what you would term seven minutes for the detail and the lower jaw, for this was to represent man who was to speak with its mind and its mouth both. Know also that in the languages and the number systems prepared for this Earth, there was a direct connection with the implementation of specified sequential growth with these languages, numbers and symbols. All of this is coded into the Skull. All of this remains to radiate out to any who listen.

As the two were prepared, it was important that they both came from pieces of crystal needed for this purpose so that the vibratory action of the Earth was similar in both of them. Thus, as they are in total connection and have been for approximately four million years, there is in the whole of the action now the unfolding or radiating in measured understandings from that skull in Sirius and to the Skull upon your Earth, giving to it the task of moving in balance and force at all times for the totality of vast growth in the human race.

The first time was a short time in which your Earth was seeded to produce all crystals that abide in your world now. Also, the first time, the image of the Skull was placed in the core of the Earth with the resonating force for the direct connection.

The group of ten have worked, lived, functioned, and operated in all capacities upon the physical Earth and upon many other physical earths and other earths. So you see, the answer is not simple. For it was with the combined action of the dedication and love and willingness of ten to come together in a circle and do the creating. Nameless, yet Masters of Light in all realms.

Your next question.

Was the Crystal Skull formed of one piece of crystal, and if so, did it come from Calaveras County in California?

There were three places upon the Earth in which seeds of this particular crystal were placed to grow, not in what you know to be your physical, dark soil, but to grow in what you would call a combination of air-water. The chosen pieces for these two skulls came from what you now call California, which was part of a vast land-mass area under creation for many millions of years. It was that it was grown at a particular meeting of energy lines and points of joining in a crystal webbing design that lies about and upon the Earth. Yes, you can say it came from there, yet it came from a particular energy field created by the crossing and the meeting of lines and spaces. This is in accordance with what you know to be the poles and the movement in relation to all planets, and especially to your Sun.

Go on.

How long did the crystal grow in the Earth before it was fashioned into the Skull?

What you would term a million years, created from a seeded point, a piece that grew according to the pulsations and the waves and the actions of the Earth in its formation. The piece was large because there were imperfections in part of it.

Who placed the seeded crystal in that portion of the Earth?

In the knowingness of man, there has always abided in and upon this Earth forms of man. The seed, placed by what you would term the essence of One, or God, or the Creator of forms of and understandings who was yet birthing many forms needed on this Earth. The knowing of the three seedings was done in the Mind of pure Light, placed at specific positions and held there in the energy forms that cradled it as it grew. The form of what you term God is the Beingness of All and includes the Beingness of your physical Earth, thus your working in union in the knowing and in the image that which needed to take place takes place automatically.

As these things are done, there are light forms of understanding that you might call angels who watch over particular creations upon this Earth; who know their full formation, the time, the space, the purpose and the All so that all things are accomplished in the transformation of the human race.

How many life-sized, real crystal skulls are there on the Earth?

There were created in succeeding moments of need, 13. These vary in size and completion. Know that in the rhythmic wave movement of light of essence through the human race, the movement itself creates and holds a form of the creating which the humans accomplish in various cycles. Different skulls represented different cycles of growth. Incomplete, or smaller, or more complete, depending upon the accomplishments of humans in the whole capacity of knowing, understanding, and expression. They reflected not only massive growth change, but direct stoppage of growth at times. They are placed at specific points around the Earth which have need of the vibrations that emanate from them in their space. They participate in the growth of the race for the people in that area. The Skull that abides in what you term North America is what you would call an example of Grace, and the crowning joy of the total completion of the human race to be accomplished in what you would call the next century, approximately 2150.

Of the 13, those that are yet undiscovered hold the possibility that they will not be discovered until the next century. This is in accordance for the position in the Earth where they now abide. What the Earth has need of and what man wants holds a different vibration, and the Earth is served first because it is the Earth that supports the human transformation. The two are hand in hand.

Go on.

Can you indicate where these other skulls are?

They lie in what you would term patterns of the topmost and bottommost points of octahedrons, centered at the equator equally around the Earth. Envision four huge octahedrons and you will have the approximate positions of eight. Four of these are of a crystal that is from what you call near the North Pole. Four of these are of crystal which grew near the South Pole. Now as you know poles and movement, these were not always north and south, but they were in specific relationship in the space between Sirius, the Sun and this Earth. There are those that are known in museums, and these are correct. There are no more in the Earth to be discovered, for it is not necessary in the balance and in the maintaining of the movement of the Earth for any others to be prepared and placed.

These formations around the Earth are

both what you would term etheric and physical formations of the Crystal Skull. They can be in the etheric and not maintain a formation in or upon your physical Earth. The number that is necessary to be remembered is that which the Skull speaks about. The radiance of the whole of one mind. One form, one essence, one teaching, one perfection. This is where humans return into this understanding.

Go on.

Was this Skull really found at Lubaantun, or was that just a publicity story? If so, where was it really discovered in the '20s?

Yes, man in his creation creates to cover up, and then creates to uncover. So, this Skull appeared in the room of the man who was proceeding to do his part in uncovering what was to become a treasure of the human race.

The man had a dream about the Skull. Information was opened to him. He became obsessed with the finding of the Skull. Before he was to proceed to the place where history says it was found, it appeared and rested on a stand by his bed. He, being waked from a sound slumber by the sound and the emanation of it, was placed in what you would term an altered state for several hours while the Skull spoke to him, and while his body was altered so that he could tolerate the presence of the Skull to accomplish what needed to be done.

He was both awed and terrified of it. It spoke to him constantly, when he awoke and when he went to sleep. He did not realize that he could communicate and answer it. He simply waited to be told what he was to do with it, because there were understandings in him that wanted to bury it forever, and there were understandings that spoke to him about holding it in great reverence, because its appearance upon this Earth had to do with the maintenance of the Earth in its wholeness through specific changes.

He agreed to maintain it, and to keep it with him. He told no one, not even the daughter. The Skull would present itself in the physical when it spoke to him when he was alone. When he traveled, and when he was active with other humans, it was not in sight.

He was sent to that particular area of the Earth because it represented and held forms of himself which he needed to uncover. And in the process of his own uncovering, the Skull appeared in the spot where it was found by his daughter. It was as much a surprise to him as to her, for he hadn't seen it for many days. In his awareness he knew that he was to do that which came to them to do with it—which he did.

There were times when it would be connected and activated from Sirius, and also from the Pleiades with thought, and Arcturus with thought, when it would change color by itself and each color had a different sound. And sometimes the sounds woke him, and other times they put him to sleep.

He became afraid of what it would do next. He didn't know that it was communicating with him through the color, connecting energy fields upon the Earth wherever the Skull was to be for the purpose of balance and teaching and demonstrating. He became more afraid of it than enjoying it. His desire was to remove it so that it would not emanate its sound to people anymore. Part of this was because he had memories of other Times and Spaces in which it was revered and in which it was feared and used as a control form.

The Skull abides where it has need of abiding. It travels where it has need of traveling for the activation of points upon the Earth, especially in the United States.

Go on.

How many years did Mitchell-Hedges have the Skull before it was rediscovered in Lubaantun? And where did it appear to him? Where was he when it appeared to him?

He was in what you would term Egypt when it first appeared. It appeared to him in England. It appeared to him in the Southwest, the area that you would term Arizona, New Mexico. He had, or was possessed by, in a sense, as he thought, the presence of the Skull for three years. It would be with him and teach, and then it would not be there. This was only a matter of using thought to accomplish this. The Skull in its own capacity knows what it is to do, and maintains itself in the doing.

Go on.

Was the Skull ever used in active magic? If so, please explain.

In the process of activating minds, there are ways of implanting thoughts from what you would term the ether form into the human form capacity. There has been a cleavage. Would you please repeat your question.

Please explain how the Skull was used in active magic.

In the forms and the forces that guided what you know to be the Magi and the wise men who studied the Vedas, and in the form and force of what you know to be Central America, the Indians that are called Mayan revered and used the Skull as it appeared to them, known and unknown by the priests and the guiding factors at that time was the reality that at times the Skull was a projected form that appeared and felt physical and was not physical at all. And sometimes the Skull was in its physical form.

The difference lay in what the intentions of the priests and the teachers were. For the Skull could literally resonate tones as it was focused in the minds of the Masters as they functioned with

Masters upon the Earth.

The Skull was used as a form of teacher, and as a form of God. Magic, yes, because the forcefield literally filled the area for hundreds of miles when it was in its physical state that it abides in now, and when it was triggered and the receiver of thoughts sent on laser beams for the rapid growth of the humans at that time to bring into the human consciousness the culture, the understandings, the capabilities, and the wisdoms of many times.

The magic of the Skull was used at specific times of the years as a point of celebration, and as a point of total reverence, especially when there were eclipses and when there were storms and cataclysms of great nature, the Skull was then used as a symbol of the radiance of the Sun. This helped people, but it also frightened people.

Specifically, what you would call rituals of magic were done at the time of the Full Moon. This was when the Skull image would appear to be physical and feel to be physical, yet it was a transfer of sound that was used. This was used by the teachers, the masters, and the priests—not always in unified action, and not always to teach the Light that exists, the power that lives whether you see it in one form or whether you see it in countless other forms.

It was control, yet it was control over the

humans for a massive regrowth and reimplanting of wisdoms within the physical stature of
what you know to be humans.

In this way, thousands of years could be
accomplished in a short while. For in the ceremonies of magic with the Full Moon, all people
participating and observing the Light radiating
through the Skull would be transported into an
other vibratory rate in which they would learn,
or in which they would sleep, according to their
own need.

Thus, a service, as you might term it now,
or a ritual experience or expression, could take
three hours, and the human would emerge after
that with greater capacities, and with understandings that they did not have before. This
was in its positive use. This can yet be in the
positive use through the mind of human, being
the essence of all Light.

Rituals—that word for particular cycles of
growth in both male and female—did not use
the Skull, but the memory of the Skull lived in
the people for all time. The humans scattered
upon the Earth now who participated in that
massive reimplanting and blooming expression
of wisdom are now also touched by the sound of
the Skull, whether they realize it or not, for it is
the Skull calling to the nature of One Light, calling it from out of the depths of every human.
This is part of its capacity and task.

Go on.

Does Phyllis have a connection with the Crystal Skull? If so, what is it?

You observed and participated in ceremonies in the role of priestess and in the role of priest. You understood many capacities of the Skull. It fascinated you; you were not afraid of it. You followed it in your memory into different Times and Spaces as you did what could be called astral traveling, always searching, bringing forth understanding, which you do yet. It is a friend. It is a teacher, and you are doing your part now in disseminating understanding and feelings to go out to many people to reaffirm the silent calling which the Skull itself is doing.

It began resonating to a much greater degree 30 years ago, and each period of ten years it increases its resonance. Set for, and participating in the stages of development of humans, it continues its work.

Go on.

What geographical area was Phyllis in when she actually saw the Crystal Skull?

You saw it in a vision in Egypt in what you would term the very early ruling dynasties. You saw it in what you would term South America, as its image was brought into a cavern where there was much activity connecting humans of the Earth and humans of other Earths. You saw it in Central America. You traveled with it for some ceremonies there. You are aligned in its inner energies, and this creates in you many changes. How you accept and function with these changes now will allow you to function with the crystal again, in Mind.

Go on.

Is there a connection between this Crystal Skull and Quetzalcoatl, the deity from Central America?

Yes. A connection that arises in what you term the outer planets and the stars for the spirit that abides in Quetzalcoatl is the spirit that resonates and brings forth growth in the human race. The Skull and Quetzalcoatl do similar things but on different vibratory rates for fulfilling the needs of the humans upon this physical Earth and in this physical nature.

Quetzalcoatl lives in the minds of humans and also lives in the forms and forcefields of growth and development upon this Earth. Physical nature, etheric nature, and astral nature—all of these are functioned in and emanated from the understanding of Quetzalcoatl. There shall be many changes and awarenesses of this once again.

That which lives in legend was lived in reality of the physical nature at some point and some space upon this physical Earth. That which lives in legend lives in the hearts. It is the understanding of its presence and its appearance that is important for humans to know. To know that life and spirit abide in the heart and to take wing and birth at specific times in lives is to know that the capacity to be a radiant being is a reality upon this Earth in which humans grow and developed.

What appears from thin air can appear in other ways. Many things from other times, from other needs and other Spaces, will appear in and out of this physical nature when there is need.

Go on.

When Quetzalcoatl lived on Earth, was the Skull there with him?

For a period of time it appeared and communicated with him. It brought him into communication with his brothers in the far reaches. It maintained this communication in the form of the image of the Skull. The Skull stayed, taught this, placed in resonance, and then was released into unobserved stillness again so that he could develop according to that which he came to do on all levels.

Go on.

Was the Skull fashioned from any particular person?

Not from what you call a person, but from a Form of thought of what the clarity of mind needed to attain in size and in resonance for the total expression of Being within a physical human body. So it came from the essence of its Being to demonstrate and to say to humans, "This is what you are. This is what you can develop."

Why is the Skull made of quartz?

The properties of quartz are fashioned from the air, water, creative sound that forms what you now know to be the physical Earth. The properties also contained the sound essence from the systems of Suns in all universes. Quartz has in its form and formation the capacity to transform and maintain in any space, in any place, and in any vibration; thus it was used so that the image would also be able to be used in any place, not only on this Earth but what you would term other stars, other planets, other forms of air and water, other forms of light energies. All participating in the vibratory change of the physical, human Earth emanating to the physical Earth the properties from the etheric Earth so that all things can be accomplished as smoothly as possible in the transformation in sound.

There is an American Indian legend that is similar to what these psychic interpreters have presented and may be of interest to the reader:

According to some American Indian beliefs, the Star People from Sirius inhabited our Earth some 250,000 years ago. There were 12 inhabited planets, of which Earth was the least involved, and they left their wisdom behind in several crystal skulls.

This belief goes on to say that eight great powers of the world—Jewish Cabalists, African Voodooists, Tibetans and Egyptians, Hindus and Moslems, Anglo Saxons, Buddhists, and Christians—all have 12 major skulls each.

Further, the legend states that each of these crystal skulls held a holographic memory computer of the collective conscious and unconscious knowledge and experience of a planet. There is one skull for each inhabited planet, and all 12 were codified into the central amethyst skull called "The Ark."

Chapter Thirteen

THE MESSAGE OF THE CRYSTAL SKULL

There seems to be a common thread among all who have seen the Mitchell-Hedges Crystal Skull: it *has* a message. Most agree that it represents the wisdom of humankind, that it demonstrates in a symbolic way what each of us is capable of attaining.

The Crystal Skull represents to many a storehouse of wisdom, a repository of the knowledge of the universe, just waiting to be tapped. It holds knowledge much as a computer does, and when we are capable of accessing its memory programs, all will be available to us.

(This information was again channeled from Lorraine Darr:)

Why is the Skull important to the world at this time, and how is it helpful?

As the Earth obtains specific points of vibrational change, there is directed from Sirius to this Skull to the center of the Earth, a burst of light, or as you might call it, a laser of sound which emanates in the air activating growth in the human race. The Skull is being used for this constant reactivation of forms of knowledge and wisdom which were once a part of the clarity demonstrated by the crystal, the clarity of light used by humans in a physical body.

This will be attained again, yet in the attainment there is a sequential, constant increase in the sound that is needed to activate and draw from the mind of humans all things that abide there in the stillness to be brought out.

Thus the Skull supports the growth of humans and demonstrates the clarity of mind achieved in stillness so that understanding can be absorbed from all places. And that which is needed can be drawn out, bringing the total reactivation of light in a physical, human body into a specific growth stage by certain times or periods of 50 and 100 years, as you would call them.

The Skull both fascinates and in a sense connects with the Knowingness of Being to speak within the soul any connection that an individual may have in their growth unfolding. Their awareness opens and they are drawn to pictures, books, articles, the name itself, for they are drawn to see it and feel once again that which they know to be the total possibility of the attainment in the form that is known as God-human in a physical form upon the Earth to carry the clarity of the Gods within the Skull and to maintain and emanate the radiance of Being from the heart is what humans are growing through and within.

Important, very important, for the Earth in its imaged form in the core of the Earth, the Skull aids in the movement and the directing of Light forces of this Earth for all changes.

What is to be known and accepted by humans is the fact that this Crystal Skull abides within the head of each physical body, if the individual soul and spirit unite and hold in the unity the sound of its Being. You may say, "This may never be accomplished."

What you see in a week's time or a month's time now will be done in days and moments in the coming years.

Go on.

What IS the message of the Crystal Skull?

The message resonates in the silence of its Being, just as the message of the Sphinx has resonated to the human race for thousands of years. The teaching: to attain clarity and understanding, you need to abide in stillness. The Skull continues that teaching, yet adds in the capacities of humans now.

There is the opportunity to advance in the clarity of all bodies, and to attain the clarity of mind in the stillness of your Being. Then, to live and abide as your Being resonates and lives that which is the perfect, radiant, clear, crystal understanding.

The message says, "Persevere. It is possible, and it is possible in this Time space."

A mighty clearing, yes, a mighty change of all habits and patterns, yes. A mighty acceptance of new patterns, yes. These do not need to occur through cataclysm or wars, or persecutions any longer. They can occur in the mind and the understanding of man. Holding and abiding in clear light it says, "I am what you are. Uncover and you will see the crystal clarity of your mind," and then allow it to be used for the development of humans.

To see and know and participate in thought with the Skull is to hold and maintain the universal connection of sound, light, color, and formation of Forms. And these are there now for humans to use in countless different ways, to transfer understandings from symbols, from pictures, from words, from silent thoughts into that which is needed for the total development and growth of humans in this time.

The Skull says, "You are a crystal Being. You have the capacity to teach this, to be this, to live in this. You can, I can. The possibility is there and the challenge. Do with a clear heart, for to clear the mind first is to bring the capabilities of mind into the heart to be used in a very whole, clear way. Enjoy, walk in the stature of your Being and radiate all the clarity that you can.

So be it.

If readers are interested in a personal psychic reading, Lorraine Darr may be contacted at: R.R. 2, Box 162, Westby, WI 54667

BIBLIOGRAPHY

Arguelles, Jose. *Mayan Factor: Path Beyond Technology.* Santa Fe; Bear and Co., 1987.

Muck, Otto. *The Secret of Atlantis.* New York, NY; Times Books, A division of Quadrangle/The New York Times Book Co., 1978. Translation copyright 1978, William Collins Sons & Co. Ltd.

Leon-Portilla, Miguel. *Aztec Thought and Culture: A Study of the Ancient Nuhuatl Mind.* Norman; Univ. of Oklahoma Press, 1963.

Waters, Frank. *Mexico Mystique.* Chicago; Swallow Press, 1975. Athens; Reprinted Ohio Univ. Press.

Sejourné, Laurette. *Burning Water: Thought and Religion in Ancient Mexico.* Berkeley, Shambhala Pub., 1976.

Gris, Henry and William Dick. *The New Soviet Psychic Discoveries.* Englewood Cliffs; Prentice-Hall Inc., 1978.

STAY IN TOUCH

On the following pages you will find listed, with their current prices, some of the books and tapes now available on related subjects. Your book dealer stocks most of these, and will stock new titles in the Llewellyn series as they become available. We urge your patronage.

To obtain a FREE COPY of our latest full CATALOG of New Age books, tapes, videos, crystals, products and services, just write to the address below. In each 80-page catalog sent out bi-monthly, you will find articles, reviews, the latest information on all New Age topics, a listing of news and events, and much more. It is an exciting and informative way to stay in touch with the New Age and the world. The first copy will be sent free of charge, and you will continue receiving copies as long as you are an active customer. You may also subscribe to *The Llewellyn New Times* by sending a $2.00 donation ($7.00 for Canada & Mexico, and $20.00 for overseas). Many bookstores also carry *The Llewellyn New Times*, and you can pick up a copy from your favorite store. If they are not currently carrying our catalog, ask them to write to us and we will be happy to supply them. Order your copy of *The Llewellyn New Times* today!

The Llewellyn New Times
P.O. Box 64383-092, St. Paul, MN 55164

TO ORDER BOOKS AND PRODUCTS ON THE FOLLOWING PAGES:

If your book dealer does not carry the titles and products listed on the following pages, you may order them directly from Llewellyn. You may order from our catalog or from this book. Please add 50 cents per item postage and $1.00 per order for handling (USA and in US funds). Outside USA surface mail add $1.50 per item. Outside USA Air Mail add $7.00 per item. Send orders to:

LLEWELLYN PUBLICATIONS
P.O. Box 64383-092
St. Paul, MN 55164-0383, U.S.A.

CRYSTAL AWARENESS
by Catherine Bowman

For millions of years, crystals have been waiting for people to discover their wonderful powers. Today they are used in watches, computer chips and communication devices. But there is also a spiritual, holistic aspect to crystals.

Crystal Awareness will teach you everything you need to know about crystals to begin working with them. It will also help those who have been working with them to complete their knowledge. Topics include crystal forms, colored and colorless crystals, single points, clusters and double terminated crystals, crystal and human energy fields, the etheric and spiritual bodies, crystals as energy generators, crystal cleansing and programming, crystal meditation, the value of polished crystals, crystals and personal spiritual growth, crystals and chakras, how to make crystal jewelry, the uses for crystals in the future, color healing, programming crystals with color, compatible crystals and metals, several crystal healing techniques, including the Star of David Healing. This book is destined to be the guide of choice for people who are beginning their investigation of crystals.

0-87542-058-3, 200 pgs., illus., mass market format $3.95

CRYSTAL HEALING: The Next Step
by Phyllis Galde

Discover the further secrets of quartz crystal! Now modern research and use have shown that crystals have even more healing and therapeutic properties than has been realized. Learn why polished, smoothed crystal is better to use to heighten your intuition, improve creativity and for healing.

Learn to use crystals for reprogramming your subconscious to eliminate problems and negative attitudes that prevent success. Here are techniques that people have successfully used—not just theories.

This book reveals newly discovered abilities of crystal now accessible to all, and is a sensible approach to crystal use. *Crystal Healing* will be your guide to improve the quality of your life and expand your consciousness.

0-87542-246-2, 224 pgs., illus., mass market format $3.95

THE AZTEC CIRCLE OF DESTINY
Bruce Scofield & Angela Cordova

The 260-day calendar of the Aztec and Maya civilizations had been buried for centuries due to neglect and repression by conquistadores and missionaries. Now this accuarate and ancient Mesoamerican calendar and divination system has been revived by the authors using both historical research and psychic techniques.

The result of the authors' careful research has resulted in a complete and entertaining system of divination. Enclosed is a fascinating book with many unique images of the gods, sample card layouts, readings, and a complete list of associations for the calendar days. Here is a easy-to-use and helpful system of daykeeping and divination for your increased well-being.

0-87542-715-4, 256 pg. book, 13 wooden chips, 20 cards, cloth bag $19.95

THE SPACE/TIME CONNECTION
Leo F. Ludzia

Reality is not what you think it is. This fascinating book will shatter old misconceptions about the true nature of reality. You will learn about the mysterious "4th dimension" of time that is used by humanity but misunderstood.

Here are the latest scientific findings from the worlds of modern physics and mind science. Written in a fast and easy-to-understand format, it presents a model of humanity, mind and the universe that is disturbing to what we have been told is real, but is somehow familiar.

From reading this book and doing the easy exercises included, you will be able to obtain *anything you desire!* No longer will you be a victim of fate. You can gain in self-confidence, and change your life forever.

0-87542-449-X, 200 pgs., illus., mass market format $3.95